My Life
as a
Country Doctor

It's Life at its Best

Purchased 3/9/09
at Wells Kitchen in
        Brighton TN

couldnt resist the
Devil made me do it

My Life
as a
Country Doctor

It's Life at its Best

Hugh Vaughan, M. D.

Pleasant Word

Pleasant Word (a division of WinePress Publishing, PO Box 428, Enumclaw, WA 98022) functions only as book publisher. As such, the ultimate design, content, editorial accuracy, and views expressed or implied in this work are those of the author.

Unless otherwise noted, all Scriptures are taken from the Holy Bible, New International Version, Copyright © 1973, 1978, 1984 by the International Bible Society. Used by permission of Zondervan Publishing House. The "NIV" and "New International Version" trademarks are registered in the United States Patent and Trademark Office by International Bible Society.

Scripture references marked KJV are taken from the King James Version of the Bible.

Scripture references marked NASB are taken from the New American Standard Bible, © 1960, 1963, 1968, 1971, 1972, 1973, 1975, 1977 by The Lockman Foundation. Used by permission.

ISBN 1-4141-0163-5

Library of Congress Catalog Card Number: 2004103843

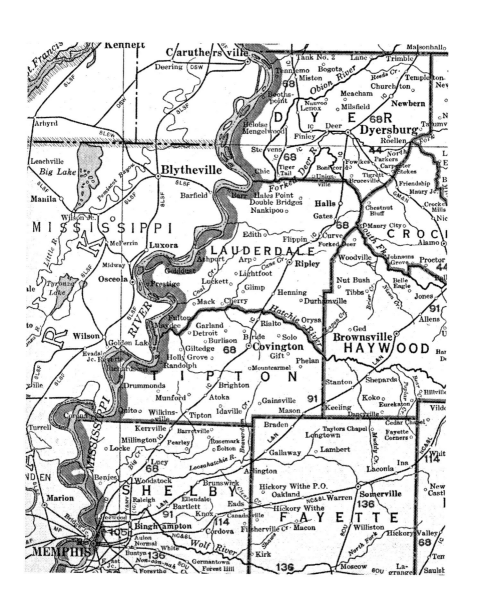

Table of Contents

Author's Notes

I hope this book of true stories about practicing medicine in the small town, country setting gives you a little insight into human nature. I also hope I am able to portray how fortunate I was to have had the opportunity to practice with Dr. Sid Witherington. I feel that no one could have had a more satisfactory life's work than mine. I shall always be indebted to the people of Munford and the surrounding area, as well as to the employees of Munford Clinic. What a great time we had! I think that a physician, his patients, and employees in a country practice become like family. This book is dedicated to Dr. Sid and the employees of Munford Clinic that I had the privilege of being with over the forty-three years and four months that I practiced.

I am especially grateful to Judy Scott Lindley for the encouragement she gave me concerning this book and helping me get it ready for a publisher. I am indebted to Sandra L. Brown, Reference Services Librarian and the University Archivist of Southwest Baptist University in Bolivar, Missouri for her immeasurable help with my book.

To my wife, Violet. I am so fortunate to have been married to her. She is a registered nurse, and she understood that you could not depend upon the clock for time and place of future happenings. She knew my time belonged mostly to my profession. She was, by far, the major raiser of our children, and I am thankful for her support and contribution to my life as a country doctor.

Hugh Wynn Vaughan, MD

Preface

This book tells how situational things that occur in the everyday practice of general medicine had meaning to me, and my reaction to them. It will let you know what thoughts crossed my mind at the time. The unforgettable memories of my forty three years and four months practice in Munford, Tennessee are partially expressed in this book. Human nature has always intrigued me.

The one-on-one patient-physician approach in the practice of medicine gives you an appreciation of the individual and introduces you to a diversity of personalities. It is most satisfying to be a part of a community, and have the feeling that the people in the community are glad you are there. The greetings you get at the post office, the grocery, the church, the restaurant, the golf course, or wherever lets you know you are a part.

Dr. Sid is like family to me. The Munford Clinic employees are just an extension of more family. We seemed to always have pleasant days. Going to work was something you looked forward to, and enjoyed year after year. The challenge of trying to figure out the diagnosis of the patient's complaint was always a welcomed occurrence. It was like trying to work a difficult math problem.

When you do arrive at the correct answer it is so satisfying, for you as well as the patient.

There is icing to this cake. It is the personal relationships you develop with people as they get to know you and you get to know them. Visiting with your patients is so rewarding. Country medicine affords this luxury.

There is no particular order of short stories as far as being in sequence in regard to calendar time. I did not keep a daily log.

I cannot imagine a better place to live, and raise a family than Munford, Tennessee.

Special Medical Things I Remember Prior to Medical School

CHAPTER 1

Gout

The first thing I recall about the medical field at all made a big impression on me. When dad would preach at one of the churches in the country, our entire family, mom, dad and us four siblings, would be invited to have dinner with a church member. This one particular Sunday, I must have been about six, Bill about eight, Mary four, and Martha two. When we entered this house and stepped from the hallway into the living/den area, there sat this man in a rocking chair with his left foot propped upon a hassock with a pillow beneath it.

His big toe looked about twice normal size to me and was very red, shiny, and even glistening. It seemed to glow in a reddish, pulsating manner. It must have hurt terribly. This man, just as we four kids entered the room, encircled his toe by reaching out with his arms and hands. He wanted to guard his toe from us. He had an anxious look on his face. He wanted to make sure none of us, by chance, bumped his toe. His foot stuck out over the hassock a little. He knew, without doubt, that a tiny bump to his toe would initiate severe pain. He let us know right off he had gout and touching it would hurt. Later, I never had any trouble diagnosing gout when the red, shiny, swollen, exquisitely tender toe came to the office.

CHAPTER 2

Scarlet Fever

When we lived at Kirksey, Kentucky I was five years old. This was in the days when you were quarantined to your room (to be by yourself if other siblings were present) until you were over the infection and did not pose a threat to spread that disease. There would be a large sign posted on the entrance to your house saying, QUARANTINED. People would know you had a communicable disease and not visit during this time. There were no antibiotics at that time. Sulfa drugs had not come into use.

Scarlet fever was a serious illness that posed a real, though uncommon, risk of death. It consisted of fever, severe tonsillitis, and a scarlet (red) rash, especially over the trunk of the body. Complications of this disease were rheumatic fever and acute glomerulonephritis (an inflammatory complication of the kidneys). Either could be fatal.

I developed scarlet fever and had to be quarantined to my room. Bed rest was a must. This was not all bad. I got special attention like I had never had before. Mom would fix me anything I wanted to eat. Neighbors would bring me extra goodies. I was pampered. My brother and sisters were jealous. I got anything I wanted. They got to talk to me through the door, but couldn't come in my room.

Chicken pox, small pox, measles, hepatitis, and mumps were diseases that required quarantining just like scarlet fever. I recovered without complications. Scarlet fever wasn't bad in my memory.

CHAPTER 3

Self-inflicted Gunshot Wound

The last part of summer, just before I would start medical school in September, I was at a local filling station listening to the conversation. People would gather there, shoot the breeze a while, and move on. The owner had a place behind his station where he would practice shooting a pistol. He was doing that this day while we sat inside yacking. He walked into the station, bent over, put the gun in the safe and sat down. He was a little sweaty and blood was on his shirt where his left hand had been. He said, "I shot myself." Talk about eyes opening up; everyone's did.

"Call the ambulance!" was yelled by one of the men and the funeral home at Halls was called to come get this man and take him to the hospital. In those days there were no emergency vehicles. There was no such thing as the emergency medical service ambulances. We lived in Gates, Tennessee at this time. Dad was the Methodist minister there.

The ambulance arrived pretty quickly. Halls was two miles from Gates. I helped load the man into the ambulance and asked the ambulance driver if I could go with them to the hospital. I wanted to see what they would do to him. I wanted to see how badly hurt he was, and if he died, I guess I wanted to see him die.

We rolled him into the emergency room. Dr. Raymond Webb was on call and was in the hospital, so he showed up right away. Dr. Webb examined his chest where the entry wound was. It was in the lower, outer part of his left chest. I was all eyes. Dr. Webb, after examining him, told the nurse to get an x-ray. This guy began to rant and rave, "I want to die. Leave me alone. Let me die." He repeated these statements several times.

Dr. Webb said in a loud and authoritative tone, almost like an order, "Shut up, and do as we say. If you had wanted to kill yourself, you would have taken better aim." That impressed me and must have this guy, because he shut up and was cooperative. His wound was not serious. Dr. Webb's handling of this patient sure stayed with me. I knew he really knew how to handle folks like this.

It is a small world. Years later, while I did hospital work at Tipton County Memorial Hospital, Dr. Webb came from Ripley, Tennessee and taught me how to do postpartum tubal ligations under local anesthesia. I did quite a number and never had any complications at all.

CHAPTER 4

Near Drowning

Another Gates happening is unforgettable. Two teenagers, a few years younger than I, and whose names have long been forgotten, came by to see if I wanted to go fishing with them in a nearby small lake. I had been in the Navy, finished my undergraduate work, and would be starting to medical school in the fall. The lake was about three miles out of town. I said, "Sure."

We arrived and put our hooks in the water. I decided to fish one area and they decided to fish another. We fished from the bank. The lake was probably about two-and-a-half to three acres and oval shaped. I was fishing on the east bank. The other two were on the west bank. They decided to swim some and stripped off their clothes down to their underwear. They would walk out on the vulcanized rubber pontoons that protruded into the lake that looked much like those the Army used to lay bridges on during the war. They would jump in and play around. It was not over your head until you were out about six or seven yards from the bank. This one teenager, who couldn't swim, jumped off close to the end of the pontoon that was furthermost out in the lake. He started thrashing around and under he went. This other teenager yelled across the lake to me, "Come here, he's drowning! Help him!"

I ran around the lake to where they were. I was scared to death. This youngest guy had completely disappeared under the water. The other person said to me, "Dive in and see if you can get him."

I replied, "You go down and see if you can get him." He was standing in water about waist deep and was just as scared as I was. I had always heard that a drowning person would pull you under with them; would grab you if they could reach you and hold on, and maybe cause you to drown. I had been told that you should knock them out with a blow to the chin and then try to keep their head above water. I had heard this all my life.

While I was taking my clothes and shoes off, I kept calling out to the other boy to dive down and see if he could get his buddy. I think I was afraid to go into the water. About this time, the face of the boy under the water surfaced. His head was back so that his chest was just beneath the water, but only his forehead, nose, and chin were visible out of the water. His head slowly sank beneath the water. It was as blue as indigo while out of the water. Air bubbles came up to the surface as he sank. We just were frozen in our tracks; scared and spellbound, I suppose.

I yelled, "Dive under there. Get him!"

He said, "You go get him." Both of us were scared spitless. I waded out to waist deep water toward the area where he went down. He had been motionless when his face was out of the water so I suppose I thought he couldn't fight me. Anyway, I dove toward that area and soon hit cold mud bottom. I felt around. Nothing but mud. I came up quickly by putting my feet on the bottom and shoving upwards. I doubt the water was over seven or eight feet deep. I was scared to swim around under the water and search for him. I looked at the other guy and said, "You try."

He was hesitant, scared like me. "You get him," he pleaded.

I was dog paddling at the time. I jack knifed and dove again. What luck! My hand hit a leg. I grabbed onto the leg, came up kicking, and pulled him only about three or four yards before

I could touch bottom. I told the other guy, "I've got him. Come on. Help me pull him out." He did. He reached into the water, grabbed his other leg and toward the bank we went. Each of us holding an ankle, we dragged him out of the water and up the bank about three or four yards. He was face up, not breathing, and was he ever bluish. Navy stuff came to mind. We quickly turned him face down, hoping gravity would prevent the need for me to perform artificial respiration. Just after we rolled him over, water began to come out his mouth and maybe even before I did anything he made a jerky cough. I told this guy who was the driver of the car to go get help. He started running around the lake to the car.

Before he reached where I had been fishing, this nearly drowned boy coughed again and again. He breathed a little between coughs and started to move some. I yelled at the other guy to wait a minute because I thought he was coming around. He came back to where we were. Without giving it any thought at all, we must have done the right thing in dragging him out of the water feet first. As we dragged him up the slanted bank of the lake, some water would automatically come out of his lungs due to gravity alone.

Very quickly, not over a couple of minutes I'm sure, the boy began to breath without gurgling, moved about some, opened his eyes, and his natural color returned. He would cough but was rapidly becoming conscious and aware. He sat up and in a few minutes was talking to us. We helped him up and we walked to the car. I don't recall how fast we walked or much else, but we drove him to his home and told his parents what had happened. He was still coughing off and on repeatedly. He spent many days in the hospital with pneumonia, but recovered with no lasting ill results.

There is a lighter side to this story. The Halls newspaper had a news article about this accident. It was subtitled, "A Methodist Minister's Son Saves a Baptist Minister's Son From Drowning." An apparent reference to the sprinkle baptism of Methodists versus the underwater baptism of Baptists.

Many years have passed since then. I would not know either of them, and I'm sure they would not know me. The boy's parents surely thanked us though. I was twenty-two at the time and just getting ready to start to medical school. I had been discharged from the Navy the past April. Occasionally, you get credit for saving lives. Whether you do or not is a different question. I always felt that God decides when someone dies. I believe I was used to help keep this boy from drowning. Had I not lucked upon a leg the second time I went down, I doubt I would have ever gone back down and tried again. Words are useless to describe the anxiety and fear that is experienced in a situation such as this.

CHAPTER 5

Why Become a Doctor?

I have often been asked, "Why did you go into medicine? When did you decide to become a doctor? How old were you when you finally made up your mind?" To be honest, I don't know the answer to any of these questions for sure.

Perhaps that had always just been my destiny. It seemed understood that when I graduated from high school I would go on to college. At that time in my life, I just did not think of any other profession to go into. When I started college I just took pre-med courses. After the first quarter and just a short while after the second quarter started, I turned eighteen and was draft eligible. I received a letter from the draft board stating that because I had entered college, and it was early in the new year, my draft status would remain open. After the first year of college was over, I would be in the June draft.

The war was over for all practical purposes, but drafting went on. Before the June draft, because I wanted no part of being a foot soldier, I joined the Navy Medical Corps with four of my college buddies. It was only two or three weeks after I joined the Navy that drafting stopped. I would not have been drafted but I'm sure you will notice all through this book that I have been lucky all my life.

Joining the Navy at this time just helped me; not only medically but financially as well. Being a Methodist minister's son enabled you to attend this small Methodist college on credit. I attended Lambuth College in Jackson, Tennessee. My freshman year was, essentially, all "charge it." I did work in the cafeteria washing dishes; and later also mopped the dorm floors, baths and stairs to help pay for my tuition and room and board. The Navy stint made me eligible for the GI Bill which ended up paying my bills for the remainder of my undergraduate courses and the first four quarters of medical school. Another chapter will deal with my dad dying at the end of my fourth quarter and how lucky I was after that regarding medical school cost.

When I went to Bainbridge, Maryland for Corps school (which was quite good) we were told that when we finished, there would be certain areas open for new corpsmen and your choice of duty would depend upon your grades. The Navy assigned the student with the highest grades to the duty of his choice. They started at the top of the class and worked down. For this reason, I tried to do especially well and was fortunate enough to finish in the upper part of the class. Because of this I was able to choose Key West Naval Hospital. I wanted to go where the weather was warm. In the fall and early winter in Bainbridge it is as cold as a wedge. My favorite thing about Bainbridge was the chow. We had good food and the chocolate milk was the best I ever drank.

My stay at Key West was about sixteen months and it was just one good day after another. I flat liked it there. I was not crazy about my two months in the diet kitchen. Grinding up meat, fixing soft diets, special diets, etc. was not my bag, but it let me know more about dietary problems. I also spent duty on the officers ward where most were not sick at all. Officers were mainly in for checkups, x-rays, back rubs, Old Grandad nightcaps, or whatever. I didn't know that officers ate with silver while we enlisted men ate with stainless steel until I hit the officers ward. All the officers I met were good to me. I guess Navy medical personnel are treated differently. There just was not the big gap between officers and enlisted men that I expected. One officer patient let me know that his car was available to me as long as he was there. I used it on occasion.

The best part of my duty at Key West was the maternity ward. I spent most of my time there. I took care of the babies in the nursery and assisted in the delivery room. For no reason that makes sense to me, I seemed to be liked a little better than the other corpsmen that worked in the nursery. I just did what I thought was expected of me. The doctors always seemed to be glad when I was on duty come delivery time. They seemed to like the way I assisted.

Episiotomies (cuts to widen the vagina) were done on prima gravida (patients with first baby deliveries). I must have cut suture, sponged blood, handed the doctors the right instruments or whatever, OK. One of the doctors, after I had helped him deliver several, said to me, "Repair the episiotomy. You have seen me do it enough." Normally my hands were as steady as a rock in a vice, but this suddenly gave me the shakes. He said, "I'll assist you." He encouraged me and I settled down enough to complete the job to his satisfaction.

I could relate stories about general medical care in the Navy that I thought were great but will end my Navy duty info with exact quotes of articles that appeared about me while I was stationed in Key West.

"Never a Dull Moment" was the heading of the first article. It read:

On the zero hour of January twenty-eighth, Mrs. Ivey casually stepped into her new Kaiser Wilhem down on Staples Street, and was driven to the USNH by her husband and father. When they entered the gate, "Pop" noticed three passengers, but when they parked outside the out patient department Pharmacist Mate Third Class Hugh Vaughn opened the back door of the car, and then there were four. He delivered baby boy Ivey at 0050 and held the fort while Dr. Bell, the MOOD and Dr. Greenburg (the OB watch) were summoned by telephone.

Dr. Greenburg had just left following an 0015 delivery, and his former patient was still on the delivery room table.

Mother and child were removed from the car to the delivery room and attended by Dr. Bell. Junior weighed seven pounds and eleven ounces.

The baby was placed in the incubator as a prophylactic measure. Both mother and baby are in fine condition. They say the father is gradually recuperating. He has the fourth son. Name, Kenneth William.

The hospital paper is *The Scalpel*. This second story appeared in the sports section of *The Scalpel*. It was headed, "Chief Bill Henderson and H. W. Vaughn, HM3 USN, Win Naval Hospital Doubles Tennis Championship." Beneath the heading this was written, "Chief W. Henderson and Vaughn, HM USN won the US Naval Hospital tennis doubles championship on the hospital court when they defeated Lt. (jg) D. W. Call (MC) USN, and D. E. Zimmerman, HM, USN, last Wednesday afternoon 6-1, 6-0."

When my stint in the Navy was over, it never entered my mind not to return to college. I was discharged a third Class Petty Officer. It just seemed natural to go back to Lambuth College and start where I had left off on my pre-medical school studies. The Navy experience just intensified my interest in medicine. It was not like, "I can not wait to be a doctor" type thing. It was more like I was where I ought to be and to just stay the course. I believe I enjoyed my undergraduate time as much as any student. It was nothing but fun. Why a doctor? It was in the cards. It seemed to me, my fate was to become an MD.

CHAPTER 6

Becoming a Doctor

Returning home after discharge in April of 1948, I had five months of leisure time before my second year of college. I became bored with the 52/20 bit (the government's military program that gave military personnel twenty dollars a week for fifty-two weeks after discharge). After three or four weeks I took off for Detroit, Michigan to work in a factory and earn a little more money. I stayed with my dad's brother and his family. I shall always be indebted to Uncle Warner and Aunt Mattie and their family. I worked at the American Aluminum Company where cylinder heads for the Nash cars were produced.

In the fall, I returned to Lambuth College and resumed my pre-med studies. I'm sure maturing some during my Navy duty was a big factor, but my grades just seemed so much better the rest of my time at Lambuth.

After I had completed the required courses for medical school I applied for admission to the University of Tennessee Medical School. I was accepted and entered medical school in September of 1950. I did not have a degree. I didn't have a high school diploma either. When we moved to Camden where I "graduated" from high school, Latin was not available. I was taking my second year at the time we moved there. At that time you were given two credits for Latin after taking it for two years. If you did not take it for two years you got no credit for the first year. I was told I could take Latin from a private teacher and get the credit that way. This was bad advice. It did not happen. I took my second year of Latin privately and passed but the principal at my high school said he could not accept that. I only had fifteen credits where sixteen were needed. I wore the cap and gown and went through the motions, but received a rolled up piece of typewriter paper at the graduation ceremony instead of a diploma. I took the college exam and got lucky. That's how I entered Lambuth College. So when I arrived in medical school, I had nothing to show for my education to that point.

Medical school has been touted as a "tough row to hoe" (very hard). In the fraternity house where I boarded, the Phi Rho Sigma, we were all in the same boat, since all members of Phi Rho were medical students. The medical and dental schools of the University of Tennessee were located in Memphis, Tennessee. It was not like going to a fine arts school where people were partying and playing to some degree most every night. Students knew they had to keep abreast or they would fall by the wayside. So although most studied regularly, all students hit the books hard during the week before exams.

As far as the toughness goes, I doubt it was that tough if you really applied yourself and liked the subjects that you needed to become a physician. I never thought of myself as being smarter than average; but, for me, medical school was no harder that high school or college. If I had a good lecturer as a teacher, I seemed to absorb things well. I quickly learned that professors quiz you on what they teach during lectures, not the pages of the text they skipped over. In histology for example, where the tissues of the body are studied under the microscope, it was easy to identify certain tissues because they looked like the pictures in the book showed them to be. When you looked at a slide of the stomach mucosa (the lining of the stomach), it looked just like the pictures in the books; the orange colored parietal cells looked as only they can look and are only in the stomach.

The fourth quarter of medical school ended just before Christmas, 1951. At that time I was ranked fourth in the class. My dad died while I was home for these holidays.

My dad, as most sons would say, was the best. We were quite poor financially. He never made over two hundred dollars a month plus a house to live in, in his life. He died in debt. Some of this was due to me. Dad would visit the University of Tennessee Medical School about every three or four weeks. I would get ready to go out of class and there he would be sitting on the back seat. He did this enough that after one year and a quarter of medical school he knew most of my classmates and they knew him. He was the only parent of a student that did anything like that. Looking back, I guess you could say he was proud of me. Several of my classmates, especially one of the girls asked me, "How come you are not as nice as your dad?"

While at home for the Christmas holidays, I was most concerned about getting to return to medical school because my GI Bill had run out. I had been to the dean of the medical school and asked about getting a loan somewhere. He said he would see if any were available and for me to come back and check with him before the next quarter started. He set a date for me to return. The banker in Gates, Tennessee, Mr. Vernon Lilly, knew dad's financial situation. I had written counter checks on dad when I had to have a little money. Most of the time it was for five or ten dollars for cigarettes and coke money. These small checks, I found out later, overdrew dad's account a lot of the time but none were returned due to insufficient funds. Mr. Lilly was the bank president. He helped us every way he could. He had told me the bankers association had given money to the University of Tennessee for student loans and there should be money available for students like me.

On Christmas day about ten o'clock in the morning, dad had chest pain, became sweaty and sort of ashen gray in color. He was quite sick. A physician from Halls, Tennessee came to the house to see dad. After his examination, he said that dad had had a heart attack. He said his blood pressure was now stable and that bed rest, pain medication, and time would let us know how he would do. The year was 1951 and in those days there was no cardiac unit in any hospital, no by-passes, no heart lung machines or anything like we have now. They did not even have recovery rooms in the hospitals in Memphis at that time. People stayed at home if they were stable. They stayed in bed for lengthy periods of time and got out of bed only to use the bath room or slop jar for excreta. No shower or bath for three days after a heart attack was standard.

We called his mother in Detroit, Michigan. She and dad's sister came via bus to see him. He seemed to be doing fine after he stabilized. On the third day after his attack, I and a buddy of mine, Bill Garrett, went to Memphis so I could again see the dean about a loan enabling me to return to medical school. I had no luck. The dean told me all loans that had been available were being used. When we returned to my home in Gates, Tennessee there was a hearse in front of the house and cars everywhere. Dad had died and mother would not let them take him until I returned. She wanted me to see him. Talk about heavy-hearted, boy, was my heart heavy. My dad had just died and I had no money to return to school. What in the world would we do? We had essentially no money and dad had no insurance. Dad was fifty years old.

I do not know to this day just how Mom managed. I do know we had a cheap casket. Dad had a sister in Kentucky that had a burial lot not far from Mayfield, Kentucky that we could use. This enabled us to have his funeral on December 31, 1951 in Gates at the Methodist church where dad had preached. We buried him in Trinity Methodist Church cemetery which was where he had preached his first sermon. His sister's family lot was there. I was born in Mayfield on January 11, 1928, where dad was employed by Railway Express before he went into the ministry.

Dad had a great tenor voice. He did evangelistic singing at revivals and churches before he went into the profession of being a minister. He received his call to the ministry, quit his good job at the railroad station, and became a circuit preacher of the Memphis Conference of the Methodist Church. His ministry started at Manleyville, Tennessee.

As you would expect, our relatives and the people of this small town of Gates felt quite sorry for us. They had heard of my plight and no loan for school. I actually was three days late starting back for it took that long to get mom moved to my brother's house and to get local debt satisfied for the moment. A second cousin of mother, Charles May, and a Mr. Ed Garrett, a Gates resident, both signed a note at the Gates Bank for enough money to get me started back and through the fifth quarter of school. Hopefully, by this time I would have secured a loan somewhere to finish school. The next quarter I dropped to twenty-second in the class. Dad's death took a toll. I ended up ninth in the class at graduation.

About three weeks after I entered the fifth quarter, Mr. Lilly of the Gates Banking and Trust Company called me and said for me not to be worried. He informed me that the bank was going to loan me the needed money each quarter until I finished school and that repayment of the loan would start when I began practice. He never did tell me who backed the loan. I always thought he did personally, but will never know for sure. After I started practice on February 1, 1955, I talked with Mr. Lilly. He said for me to pay each month what I could on the loan and not to worry, just make regular payments. I paid fifty dollars a month until the loan was liquidated. Would you say I have been blessed?

I might add, that the money loaned me was for essentials. In an effort to have a little extra cash money for dating, frat parties, renting a tuxedo for our Founder's Day banquet and the like,

I applied for, and received a job at Methodist Hospital working in the lab. I would do lab work on new admissions after I had completed my day at school. I had to finish doing lab work on all new patients that were admitted that day up until six o'clock in the evening admissions. Stat lab work (emergency work) was done anytime during the night.

I became very well known in the hospital. "Student Vaughan" was paged regularly for stat lab work and by the time I graduated eight quarters later, my name was as common as dirt. This was another example of luck falling in my lap. The hospital allowed me to live in the intern quarters for I had to be available for lab work at night. This cost me nothing and I was allowed to eat in the cafeteria at no cost.

The first six quarters of medical school were basic sciences such as anatomy, histology, chemistry, physiology, pharmacology, neurology, and the like. After these first six quarters, the University of Tennessee had you lay out a quarter. We went though twelve quarters of school in three years and three months. The lay out quarter was right in the middle. I spent this three months working at the Rutherford County Hospital in Murfreesboro, Tennessee. I worked in the ER there and assisted as a scrub nurse in surgery. It was a great experience in just seeing how different doctors went about their business. I had the opportunity during this internship to see a variety of bedside manners; some that I hoped I could use as well as others that I hoped I didn't acquire. Each doctor has his own way. I always felt comfortable talking to my patients.

The last six quarters of medical school were the clinical quarters. We began to see or be shown patients. Their symptoms and the history of these symptoms were taken or given to you with discussion of the possibilities that exist (the differential diagnosis); the patient has this illness or that disease. Needed lab work was done or discussed after obtaining the facts. We would, with the resident physician or staff physician, talk about the disease, its treatment, and its prognosis. This gave me the feeling that I was really getting somewhere now.

To see my first patient was such a thrill, yet it also made me humble as humble can be. You seem to, in the last six quarters, go over and over the basic science material as it is applied clinically. Anatomy, physiology, chemistry, bacteriology, etc. were repeated day after day. Things you had learned but half forgotten began to be implanted into your brain. Repetition of information is a very good way of remembering.

By the way, in medical school you are with the same group, (there were forty-two of us) every day. All are in the same classes and all are doing the same thing. You get to know each other pretty well. We had two girls in our class. Needless to say, they were the most popular students. We studied class notes in preparation for quarterly exams. Class notes were taken by a member of our class. Some of us took notes in the ophthalmology class, some in pediatrics, etc. These would be given to our class typist who would, in turn, give the typed notes to the classmate in charge of printing, who would print out the notes and staple them together for each lecture. This was done for all subjects. Come test time, most of us got together in groups or couples and went over our class notes. We would quiz each other on the subject matter.

I always studied with Horace Yarberry. He was our class president from the beginning. He was the only classmate, as far as I know, who was personally financially secure if he "never hit a lick at a snake" again. I don't know just how we became the closest of friends as he had everything moneywise and I had nothing. I did have a family; and family life he envied. He was an only child and his father was a physician and his mother had some health problems. Anyway, Horace and I would get together a few days before exams, go over class notes, and quiz each other on them. We would do this on each subject until we felt we would probably pass OK. I think he looked forward to these study nights. I know I did.

Horace and I also double dated a lot. He married during lay out quarter. I was best man in his wedding and he was best man at mine. He drove a beautiful Chrysler New Yorker. I'd drive on our double dates. I guess he made me pay for getting to ride in a car rather than walk or take a bus on a date. I had certainly done both. I didn't go out that much. I couldn't afford to. The last six quarters went rather rapidly and were nothing but fun. What big guys we thought we were at graduation, when the President of the University of Tennessee, Dr. Holt, who lived in Knoxville, came to Memphis and hooded us at graduation and let us know we were now MDs. Graduation day was December 14, 1953. I had my sheep skin with my degree printed on it.

I began my internship at Methodist Hospital on February 1, 1954.

I want you to know that when you are paged as Student Vaughan for two years, you are actually called Student Vaughan by the staff of doctors and the hospital staff. Once I started my internship as an MD, I did not want anymore of that Student Vaughan. After all, I was Doctor Vaughan. Interns were paged whenever they were needed for whatever floor station. I knew nurses, for instance, on Third Main Station, would dial the operator and have Student Vaughan paged if lab work needed to be done. The very first day I worked as an intern, I wanted to hear Dr. Vaughan, not Student Vaughan come out loud and clear over the loud speakers. I flat picked up a house phone in the hospital, dialed the operator, and said, "Would you page Dr. Hugh Vaughan for the emergency room please?" I quickly hung up the phone and started walking down the corridor of the hospital.

Sure enough, it came out loud and clear, "Paging Dr. Hugh Vaughan, paging Dr. Hugh Vaughan." I actually sounded like somebody. Here I was, Dr. Vaughan. I liked that sound. I went to a house phone and said, "This is Dr. Vaughan."

She said, "You are wanted in the emergency room." She never said anything to me, but I'm sure she knew the voice asking for the page. I can see her smiling about it.

I received fifty dollars a month when I started my internship. I made more than twice that much while working there in the lab part time as a student. The fifty dollars a month intern's salary was paid the first of the month if all of your charts were complete. If not done, you were not paid until they were completed. I received a raise during my internship. They raised my salary to seventy-five dollars per month after I got married on September 29, 1954. Violet, my new bride, began working at Methodist in March of that year. Her name was Violet Marea Petty. She began work on the Third Main Station. That is where I met her. Violet made eighty-five dollars every two weeks as a nurse at the hospital. My salary just paid for the duplex we rented after we got married. It consisted of a living room area, kitchen, bath , and bedroom. We lived on her salary. We were married by my brother, a Methodist minister in Munford, Tennessee. His name is William M. Vaughan, Jr. My internship ended January 31, 1955.

CHAPTER 7

How I Ended up in Munford

My brother, Bill, was the minister at Munford Methodist Church. He had been there since 1952. Dr. Albert Sidney Witherington Jr. was their doctor. Everyone called Dr. Witherington, "Dr. Sid." My brother had told Dr. Sid about me. Dr. Sid told Bill he wanted a partner and Bill told me about Dr. Sid and the Munford Clinic. I met Dr. Sid and we talked about Munford as a possibility for me. He asked if I'd be interested in working for him while he took a vacation. He told me he would pay me three hundred and fifty dollars for the two weeks he would be gone. He also said that I could sleep at the Clinic and that the nurses would help me and let me know how he did things. I had two weeks vacation coming and three hundred and fifty dollars for two weeks was more money than I thought anyone might make.

I took my vacation working for him. I lived in the clinic. People had to see me or no one, so I was kept fairly busy. I even delivered a baby while there this two weeks. (My Navy stint helped here.) When Dr. Sid returned, he made me an offer to become a partner of his in practice.

I should note that Dr. Sid had a brother that was an internist with his office in Methodist Hospital where I had been a student lab guy and where I was interning. His name was Dr. Barney Witherington. Dr. Barney knew me quite well. I was never told and never asked Dr. Sid if he talked to Dr. Barney about me, and if so, what he said. You know, I didn't even have a medical license when I worked for Dr. Sid; no liability, nothing but an MD. The license and liability were never considered when I filled in while Dr. Sid was vacationing. I didn't think about them and I'm sure Dr. Sid didn't either.

Dr. Sid offered me a never heard of deal, as far as I know, before or since. He said that if I wanted to try it out, I could come there for one year. During that year we would be full partners, splitting all expenses and income. It would not matter who the producer of the income was, it would be split fifty-fifty.

There were two conditions to this arrangement. The first one had to do with the fact that he had borrowed money to build the clinic. It was a licensed hospital. He said that my half of the payments on this debt during that first year would be money down a rat hole if I decided I did not want to stay in Munford. However, if I decided to stay, I would own that much of the clinic. He said we would arrange a suitable price for the clinic, property, equipment, etc. after a year. At that time I could purchase half and it would be ours together. The other condition was that he could say to me, "Hugh, this hasn't worked out like I thought it would." He could ask me to leave and I would have to go with no questions asked.

In return, I could say to him, "This hasn't worked out like I thought it would." I could leave and he would ask no questions.

I have never heard of a half and half partnership like this. Everything was split right down the middle. We shook hands on the deal. No papers were drawn up, signed or anything like that. The deal was sealed with just a handshake. Now, was I fortunate or not?

On February 1, 1955 Violet and I were in Munford and I started practicing medicine. We moved to Munford in a car, literally.

We had only one stick of furniture, a used television set. When we married a staff physician at Methodist gave us fifty dollars. We bought the used TV with it. Our total assets consisted of our clothes, the car, and a used TV.

Over the Christmas holidays we had been to Munford and rented a four room house that had a kitchen, bath, bedroom and living area. We had been introduced to a Mr. Harry Haddad, the owner of the general merchandise store (clothes, furniture, etc.) and a Mr. Willard Arthur, the owner of the Western Auto store. We decided to purchase our furniture from the Haddad's and our appliances from the Arthur's. This was done all via credit.

I shall always be indebted to these folks. Mr. Harry told me that I could pay for the furniture as I was able; that I could pay each month what I could afford and that if I did that or let him know if I couldn't, things would be fine. He said he was glad the town was getting a new physician. Mr. Haddad said that two things a town needs particularly are churches and doctors. I paid a little each month. I never received a statement. We bought there on credit as long as we wanted to throughout the forty-three and a half years we lived there.

Brock, as Mr. Arthur was called, and I decided on a payment schedule not unlike Mr. Haddad's as I recall. Perhaps we had a set figure here per month, but I don't recall ever getting a statement from him either. He was paid off in time just as Mr. Haddad, a little each month.

CHAPTER 8

The Practice Begins

You would think I'd recall the first patient I saw as a partner of Dr. Sid; but I don't. I can tell in this book all the things that made the practice of medicine in a small town, the best job a guy could have. Munford had about 650 people at this time. This book will let you know about us, the town and the people.

The take home pay was done in a day to day fashion. At the close of each office day, the receptionist, at that time a Miss Kate Banks, would divide the day's receipts into two equal parts. She gave Dr. Sid his fifty percent and me mine. It worked that way throughout our partnership. The first of each month we would each put equal money into the Munford Clinic account. Dr. Sid's wife, Eleanor, kept books the first two or three years we were there. My wife, Violet, took over the books after Eleanor's last daughter was born. We deposited enough money to pay the salaries of our employees for the month plus the payment due on the clinic mortgage. On about the fifteenth of the month, after all our supply bills, electric, water, etc., were in and totaled, we'd hit the kitty with enough to cover those expenses. We kept a minimal balance in this account. This was done throughout the entire partnership.

We alternated calls at night and each had a day off each week. My day off was Wednesday and Dr. Sid's was Thursday. I was always on call Thursday nights and Dr. Sid was always on call Tuesday nights. We alternated the other days and weekends. One of us would be on call Saturday night, Sunday, and Sunday night. Next week the other would do the same. It was not an every other night thing but it ended up with us each working the same number of days each month. We worked daily until all patients were seen that wanted to be seen that day. It would be dark a lot of days before we went home. Our help knew this when they were hired and no one ever complained to me when we'd have a long day. We did this for a number of years.

After a few years, we dropped the Saturday afternoon office hours and only worked in the morning. After the clinic ceased being a hospital, we decided that only one physician needed to work on Saturday mornings. Eventually, we started seeing patients by appointment. I'm not exactly sure just what year that occurred. Before that time it was "first come, first served" with emergencies taking precedence. Cuts, broken bones, and women in labor were seen immediately. The appointment patients just waited.

When I started working there, Dr. Sid asked me if I would see all the OB patients and as many of the pediatric patients as the receptionist could head my way. He preferred to see as many geriatric patients and internal medicine problems as he could. He did all things and delivered babies on his night of call, but during the day I sewed up cuts, delivered the babies and put on the casts. We just drifted into this arrangement and it worked well. It was a way of getting me known and started and at the same time allowed him to spend more time with internist-like problems.

The clinic was open twenty-four hours a day, period. Holidays and all. Office hours were from nine o'clock in the morning until noon and from one o'clock in the afternoon until whenever. Closing time was considered to be five o'clock in the evening, but this rarely happened. These same hours were used Monday through Saturday. We had no office hours on Sunday, but the doctor on call would have to go see anyone who wanted to be seen. I shall never forget my busiest Sunday. On that day, I saw, in the clinic plus house calls, thirty-three patients. This was outrageous, but it happened. We had to make house calls most mornings before office hours, during lunch, and after office hours for many years. I had to see a patient at the clinic or on a night house call each and every night I was on call for over thirteen years. I always kept the phone on the floor by my side of the bed so when it rang at night I could answer it without waking Violet. One morning, I suddenly awoke and realized that I had not heard the phone ring or gotten up during the night. In a state of panic, I thought, *The phone must be off the hook!* But when I checked, it was not. Then I thought that I had answered the phone, was supposed to go to the clinic, but had fallen back to sleep and no one could get me. None of this was so. After thirteen-plus years, I had had a night on call when I did not have to get up. I slept all night. No one had called!

Chapter 9

Treasured Comments From Patients

I have always liked the unasked for comments that people make out of the blue and the candidness of what they say. The following are examples.

A lady in her late fifties was looking at my class graduation picture that was made in 1953. Without hesitation she said, "You know, Dr. Vaughan, you used to look pretty good."

Another was a male patient. I had seen him numerous times over the years as a patient only. He did not know any of my family personally. He was from one of the outlying communities. Anyway, I supposed he had talked to someone that not only knew me but knew about my family. On this particular day, after I had examined him he said, "Dr. Vaughan, you must be smarter than I thought you were. I hear you have two sons that are doctors." Human nature at work.

I have always known that when you were seeing a patient, they were to be your main focus, but that doesn't mean I practiced that all the time. When I first started practicing medicine, I would answer the phone when anyone called me. Our receptionist would buzz me and tell me who was on the phone and that they wanted to talk with me. I would stop interviewing my patient sitting there or stop in the middle of an exam to answer the phone and talk to whoever was on the other end. It took me longer than it should have to realize that your present patient is paying you and that you should be taking care of them, not giving free advice to someone on the phone.

One employee let me know that my last patient told them that my talking on the phone like that was not professional and it just wasn't nice. As a result, I advised my staff to tell patients that I would return their call. The only exceptions were if my wife, mother, or another physician phoned. One day, while I was examining a patient, another physician phoned and I excused myself from the patient and answered the phone. The patient did not know that it was another physician I was talking to and we talked, and talked, and talked. Medical terms were used frequently and I'm sure the patient knew I was in no hurry to get back to her. She was sitting nude behind the paper drape dress sheet on my examining table. She could see my back as I was sitting at the desk talking.

After too long a time, it dawned on me I had been talking for awhile. I quoted a prescription formula for a salve to the guy on the phone and said, "That's what I use." My dermatologist son, Keith, had told me this prescription. As soon as I hung up, I knew that I needed to comment about being on the phone so long, so I did not give her a chance to say anything. I quickly said, "I want to apologize for being on the phone so long. That was a doctor from the Mayo Clinic calling me to find out what I used for a certain type contact rash." She never said a word, just looked very surprised. This lady was from another town and didn't know much about me or my family. After the exam, she dressed and was ready to go when I said, "I wasn't lying, that was a doctor from the Mayo Clinic in Rochester, Minnesota on the phone. It was my son." Andy is an internist on the staff there. She looked even more surprised, smiled, and seemed to appreciate my humor. She complimented me on having a son at Mayo. She had not known about my doctor sons.

I wish I could recall the name of the lady that came to my office one day and told the receptionist that she needed to talk to me, not as a patient, but personally. I'd like to give her credit for it is one of those things you never forget. She was sent back to my office. She told me the Lord had told her to come and talk to me. I'm here to tell you, that will shake you up a bit. Flashes of thought ran through my mind quickly. I wondered what in the world I had done.

In the past, I had been told by an older man that he saw me with my arm around Miss Kate, our receptionist at that time, at Dr. Sid's father's funeral. I was sitting next to Miss Kate and I must have had my arm on the back of the bench on which we were sitting. Anyway, this type thing entered my mind quickly. I couldn't imagine what in the world she was going to say. Then she said, "I don't know how to tell you this. It sounds strange, but the other day I saw you driving your pickup and the Lord said to me, 'Go tell him he is not alone.' That's it," she said. This did seem strange to me. I wondered what it meant other than that she meant that God was with me wherever. I related this to my family. All my children were married and gone. My youngest daughter Shelley, not long after I told her this story, sent me a picture of an ocean shore scene with a lighthouse on rough terrain with whitecapping water in the background. The caption said, "Through the storms, you do not walk alone."

Country practice sure had some advantages that I doubt are present in a city practice. I do not believe people are as free to talk to their physician in a city as they are in the country. When I would refer a patient to a specialist in Memphis, it would be a common occurrence for them to return to the office and ask me to call the specialist and ask them a certain question. They did not feel free to do this directly.

Mrs. Anna Gross, who worked for us at the clinic at night while Munford Clinic was a licensed hospital called me and said that a Mr. James Black had come in and wanted to be seen. I told her I'd be there shortly. I walked into the clinic and there sat this man I knew well, but his name was not James Black. It was James Knight. This stuck with me like glue. I am bad at remembering names. You know, you think of night as dark or black. They are similar in meaning. Here,

James Knight comes in and Knight...night...black caused her to say Mr. Black, I'm sure. It is surely something I would do. Even though this amused me, I never mentioned it to her.

Mrs. Gross on another occasion made a comment that is human nature personified and represents realities in life. Her mother had Alzheimer's disease and had had this for a number of years. In those days most liked for you to call it hardening of the arteries. Anyway, it was dementia to a marked degree. I doubt she even knew her daughter. She would strip all her clothes off and walk down the road. She would play in the commode water and numerous other unexplainable things, some of them most embarrassing. When Mrs. Gross was talking to me one day, she said in a most understandable manner, "You know, Dr. Vaughan, I'll almost be glad when mama dies." This is one of the most normal statements you'll hear under circumstances such as this. At that time I didn't think anything about it except to realize that I would probably feel the same way were I in her shoes. Apparently, Mrs. Gross thought more about it; for about a year later when her mother died she came to me at the visitation wake and said, "Dr. Vaughan, I'm so sorry I told you that I would almost be glad when mama died." With tears rolling down her face she continued, "Even though she was not really like my mama, I hate to lose her." She felt some guilt. I tried my best to let her know she had no reason to feel sorry. Her mother had become no actual pleasure to herself or anyone else.

Mrs. Gross was a dear lady that loved everyone. She had all the clinic staff at her home for country cooking on numerous occasions. She had lost a son in World War II and carried on with grace. I have a deep appreciation for Mrs. Gross and people like her.

CHAPTER 10

An Intentional Compliment

Many women like to talk about their medical conditions and will not hesitate to tell you about their obstetrician or pediatrician. I was sitting at a dinner meeting where there were several people I did not know. They were sitting at the same long table. The women seemed to know one another.

One, obviously, did not know I was a general practitioner and was most talkative about her pediatrician. She told all about how wonderful he was and that there was not another doctor who could compare to him. A lady I knew well was sitting directly in front of this talkative lady. I had delivered one of her children and had seen all of her children after I arrived in Munford. She had had three children before I started practice there. She looked this lady straight in the eyes and said very confidently, "There sits (she pointed to me) the only pediatrician I ever used." She let this lady know that her children had done just fine being treated by a local MD. I felt very complimented. And as a small town doctor I was privileged to be both the obstetrician and the pediatrician.

The lady that complimented me was the wife of the funeral home owner and director. Her name was Evelyn Baddour.

CHAPTER 11

The Unintentional Compliment

One of the best things about a small town practice with small communities a few miles out in all directions as a drawing area, is that you see different-type patients and different ethnic groups. I had the good fortune to have Afro-Americans as a part of my practice. One of my patients, Ulair Brown, gave me one of the best compliments I ever received and I do not believe he intended it to be a compliment.

He was in his upper seventies or early eighties and had been a loyal patient for a number of years. This particular day he was in one of the exam rooms sitting on the table when I entered. I said, "Hey, Ulair, what can I do for you today?"

He just sat there for a second or two, then he sort of stared at me square in the eyes with an inquisitive look on his face and said, "I don't understands you."

I replied, "What do you mean, you don't understand me?"

He said with his slow, southern drawl, "I was feeling so (the so was like sooo) bad at home last night and this morning and still felt bad in the waiting room and now you come in here and I feel better already and you ain't done nothing yet." It was as if just seeing me had made him feel better and that didn't make sense to him if you are sick. I took this as an unintentional compliment.

I can tell you for sure, I felt better after seeing Ulair that morning.

CHAPTER 12

My Son Walks While on a House Call

I hope I have made it apparent throughout this book that practice in the country has the big advantage of allowing a doctor-patient relationship that I feel is lacking in the city. Our oldest son, Hugh Jr., was around a year old, but had not walked on his own. I was called to make a house call on a Mr. Sy Murphy, who lived about five or six miles from Munford. Violet and Hugh Jr. went on the call with me. Violet and the kids did this often. They got to be with me as well as see the countryside.

Upon arrival, I went into the Murphy's house. They lived in a very modest, small, frame home. I checked Mr. Murphy and gave him prescriptions. I then told them I wanted them to see my boy. You know, we always want to show off our kids. I went to the car, got him, and took him into the house. While sitting there I told them he had not walked on his own yet, but was getting close. I stood him up and held his hands to balance him. I wanted to show them he could stand alone a little. When I felt Hugh Jr. was fairly stable on his feet, I turned his hands loose, backed up, and bent over and held out my arms for him to maybe take a step and come to me. He started to step so I backed up and he stepped again. This time I backed up a couple of steps. He walked all the way to me.

This was the first time he had walked. The Murphy's enjoyed it as much as I did or so it seemed to me.

This incident became the building block for a good friendship. Not long after this, Mr. Murphy called and asked if I would like to go fishing. I went with him and we did this more than once. Not only that, but they invited us to come eat supper with them. The great thing about this kind of relationship is the closeness that develops between you and your patients. Also, you cannot beat country home cooking: chicken and dressing, peas, corn, mustard greens, tomatoes, homemade pies, etc. Country practice is quite filling and fulfilling in more ways than one.

CHAPTER 13

Word of Mouth Is the Best Advertisement

O rthopedics was not only interesting to me, but it didn't take me long to find out you were paid better for orthopedic work than for other aspects of medicine. Casting a fractured forearm or fractured ankle gave you much more profit, for cost of material and time spent, than you received in the general practice of medicine. I had good training in this field during internship in the offices of Moore, Moore, Whittemore, and Hay. I have always been grateful to them.

Not long after starting practice with Dr. Sid, a lady from Bolton who had heard of Munford Clinic, came to the office. She complained of shoulder pain and could hardly move her arm without pain. She was quite tender over the front and side part of her shoulder. She had an anterior lateral tender point, which meant to me she had a bursitis or tendonitis. I thought an injection with a steroid would help, as this is what the orthopedic group did for patients with similar presentations. I thought, *I might as well get my feet wet.* I decided that I would deaden the area with local anesthesia (carbocaine), then inject one cc of an articular steroid into the tender area. I did this and after I injected it, I just jabbed the needle in all directions under the skin to spread the steroid out.

One would think that doing this injection technique would make them so sore the next day that they really would have shoulder pain; but not so. I had instructed her in the exercises I wanted her to take after twenty-four hours and told her that I needed to see her again in three or four days. She returned and surely made my day. She could use that arm any way she wanted. She thought that I was a miracle worker. I told her to continue the exercises for two more weeks and let me see her again if she still had trouble. I did see her again for a pregnancy, but as I say, "Lucky me" because her shoulder was not a problem again.

Bolton must have been "Shoulder Pain City!" I am sure that over the next two years I saw at least ten people from Bolton with shoulder pain. All because this patient must have told people that I cured her or something like that. Word of mouth was the only advertisement you had in those days. In fact, advertisement via radio, TV, and in the newspaper was frowned upon and not considered professional. It was such a wrong thing for the medical profession to do that it was almost considered illegal. Dr. Sid and I never advertised. We didn't even have professional name cards to hand out. The Methodist Hospital system furnished me some the last four years I practiced but I never used them. Word of mouth, even still, is the best advertisement.

CHAPTER 14

Beware the Crazy 'Wish of Death'

I have always been a very opinionated guy, but I could back up my opinions with solid, hard facts about the way I felt. There have been two occasions in my life when I jokingly thought that I wished a particular person would die. You know, then I would be vindicated or whatever.

Estes Kefauver was never one of my favorite politicians to say the least, although he was a fellow Tennessean. I felt like he would say or do anything to get a vote and get elected. He would jump on everyone's bandwagon, and say he would, in essence, rid them of whatever in their lives they disliked. We all like money so Mr. Kefauver felt that if he could save people money, he could probably count on their vote.

I never shall forget how Mr. Kefauver jumped on the price of prednisone. Prednisone is a widely used steroid and a great drug. I don't recall the exact per tab price it was at that time in the United States; however, he made a big issue of how the drug companies in the US were making a killing on it when it could be bought in Mexico for a nickel a tablet. At the same time, Mr. Kefauver never mentioned the high cost of research in the US and the cost of labor in our country compared to the cost of labor in Mexico. I could talk a long time about this type of thing, but you can pretty much get the point I am making. I knew he was not being objectively honest about the total cost at all.

Probably over a year later, Mr. Kefauver suffered a heart attack and I jokingly thought, *He ought to just die.* Guess what? He did. I have to tell you that I did not feel very good about his death.

As a new doctor in town and practicing with a Dr. Witherington, it was sort of rough getting started. The local people just felt that they had not been seen by a doctor unless his last name was Witherington. Dr. Sid's dad, Dr. A.S. Sr., had practiced here in Munford, and Dr. Sid's grandfather, Dr. J.B. had practiced here before him. My patients were just used to seeing a doctor who was at least a member of this family. In 1955 when I came to this community, most of the older folks had seen doctors since the days of horse and buggies, and they all had the name, Dr. Witherington. Dr. J.B. had two physician sons, Dr. A.S. Sr. and Dr. Jack. Dr. A.S. Sr. also had two physician sons, Dr. J.B., who practiced in Memphis and Dr. Sid, who was my partner. Dr. Jack had one son who became a physician and did general family practice in Covington, another small community in our area. Dr. Jack had originally practiced in Munford with Dr. A.S., Sr., but later moved to Covington, and still practiced there in 1955. His son, Dr. Jimmy and Dr. Warren Alexander were also in practice with him at that time.

The above information leads to the patient I was called to see in Drummonds. They called for Dr. Sid, but since I was on call, they had to settle for me. This was an elderly patient with an acute illness that I felt was serious enough to demand hospitalization as soon as we could get transportation. In my medical opinion, the patient was suffering from an abdominal aneurysm that was beginning to dissect or an acute gall bladder. Either way, emergency surgery would be required.

Because abdominal pain was such a dominant symptom (in general, elderly patients complain less of pain than younger people),

I advised the family that I was going to give the patient a shot for pain. Since the patient was older, I administered 20-25 mg of demerol along with 25 mg of phenergan. At that time there was no such thing in our area as ambulance service, so the local funeral home director transported emergency cases to and from hospitals in the hearse. I advised the family I would return to the office and make arrangements for the funeral home director to pick the patient up in Drummonds and transport her to Methodist Hospital in Memphis. I would also notify the Methodist ER about her situation and inform them of the suspected diagnosis and the treatment that I had administered. After doing these things, I returned home.

To my surprise, a family member of this patient was waiting for me when I arrived at the office the next morning. He gave it to me with both barrels, He bitterly proceeded to give me all kinds of verbal abuse because I had gotten them so upset and made them believe that this family member was very sick. He stated that they had refused ambulance service and were able to get another doctor they knew to come out and see the patient. This doctor had seen the patient about an hour after I did. Pain was by then not much of a problem since the demerol I had administered had taken affect. The patient stated that she only felt achy and had vomited and felt much better. The second doctor advised the patient and her family that she would probably be OK. He suggested that the patient probably had the flu and to wait and see how she did. I have never taken a verbal beating like that one before or since.

Needless to say, I felt horrible. Had I really made such a mistake in diagnosis? I needed encouragement or sympathy or something. So, I just walked into Dr. Sid's office and told him my story. After listening patiently, he said, "I wouldn't worry about it if I were you. Dad and Uncle Jack used to see the same patient at times. One would always diagnose one thing and the other would usually come up with a different diagnosis. It became a joke between them and they would accuse each other of not knowing what they were doing."

I guess it helped to hear that, but my feelings were still hurt and I thought to myself, *I hope that old lady dies.* I truly did not mean this, but I suppose I wanted to be right. I felt I needed vindication. That entire day is etched in my memory as a day of feeling so down that I could hardly look up.

Again the next morning, upon my arrival at the office, the same man was waiting for me. However, this time he had tears in his eyes. He apologized profusely for all the things he had said to me the previous day. He also told me that the patient had died during the night of what they called an acute abdominal disorder. "She had a bad pain in the stomach," he said. He told me that I must have been right and how sorry they were that they had not listened to me. I tried to reassure him, as best I could, that because of the age of this patient, she might not have even survived the surgery if they had taken her to the hospital at the time I suggested. I told him how fortunate I thought the family was for having this member live so long.

To this day, I have never wished for another person to die, even in my thoughts. I have been ready for some to die. Those patients with terminal metastatic cancer everywhere, with pain almost impossible to control and no hope for improvement were the hardest to treat. I just tried to keep them comfortable and fed via tube feedings. Some patients with a generalized spread of cancer just wasted away to skin and bone before they succumbed to their illness. It was this type patient that you were ready for them to die. It seemed a relief.

CHAPTER 15

Dying: a Relief?

One of my patients had a hysterectomy (uterus removed) a few years before I became her doctor. She had not had her ovaries removed because she said the doctor felt a sudden "change of life" would be unpleasant for her. This was not uncommon, though I always felt that ovaries should be removed at the same time and hormone replacement therapy begun. Anyway, during yearly exams she refused pelvic examinations because she said, "I don't have anything there and I'm not having any rectal problems." Women, especially back then, were reluctant to have rectal and pelvic exams. I suppose they were embarrassed to a degree and did not even like the thought of having it done. I always thought that the fact that they knew bowel material would be encountered on rectal exams was one of the reasons for their reluctance. As a matter of fact, I always tried to get feces on my gloved finger so a hemoccult (test for blood) could be done.

This particular visit was for abdominal pain that was cramping off and on, and quite severe. It was associated with vomiting. Bowel sounds were increased and a crescendos tinkle could be heard at the height of her pain. These findings suggested bowel obstruction, and this was confirmed by x-ray. She was referred to a surgeon where exploratory surgery revealed she had rather far advanced carcinoma of the ovary as the cause of her obstruction.

Now, with metastatic disease that involved both large and small bowel, definitive surgical removal was not possible. Palliative surgery was done to relieve her obstruction. Recurrence of obstruction in these cases is quite common and three months later she had to have surgery again. By this time, she was aware that her prognosis was poor and that another obstruction would probably follow.

The pain of ovarian cancer with abdominal metastatic disease is quite debilitating and depressing both for the patient and the doctor. The physician knows that regardless of what is done, there will be essentially no long term benefit. Even long term pain relief is difficult. She talked with me freely and said, "I do not want and will not have any more surgery." She advised me that she had discussed this decision with her husband and she knew that it would be best for all concerned.

I did not feel ill at ease in saying to her, "I know from what you have said that you know you do not have long to live. What do you think about?" I was actually quite curious.

She said, "You think, why me?"

Sure enough, a few weeks later another bout of obstruction occurred and she came to my office and said, "No surgery," in the presence of her husband. "Put me in the hospital and keep me comfortable."

Insertion of a long Miller Abbott tube sometimes helps small bowel obstruction and occasionally relieves it. Insertion of this tube did not help her. Feeding was a problem. IV's are OK for a few days but are not the answer to chronic bowel obstruction. Relief of pain is difficult and requires heavy doses of narcotics. All of her medication had to be given intravenously, by subcutaneous injection, or by intramuscular injection. In an effort to help nutrition, proctoclysis was used as a manner of feeding. This involves absorbable liquids being injected via a tube into the rectum and up into the large bowel. Her condition deteriorated progressively, with hydration and pain relief becoming major problems.

To keep her pain free, I had to slug her with much larger doses of morphine than I thought patients would tolerate. I felt she would not live longer than a few more days and decided upon a conversation that I had used with other terminally ill patients. I told her, "I do not feel things are going well at all, and if you have anything you want to say to your husband or kids, I would do it in the next few days."

She thanked me and said, "I would like to talk to my husband." I do not know what she said to her husband or their children but there seemed to be a relief on all their faces. She died two days later. Her death, though sad, was a relief of a miserable existence for both her and her family. I could not be sorry when she died.

There is no way to know absolutely, but a routine pelvic exam may have picked up on an enlarged ovary prior to the spread of this disease, while it was still encapsulated. Surgery then could possibly have resulted in a cure. I recall picking one up on a patient that was about two-thirds the size of a baseball that was still encapsulated. She never had any spread at all and was doing well at least twenty years later. This says two things to me. First, you will not die of ovarian cancer after a hysterectomy if both ovaries are removed at the same time and secondly, women should have yearly pelvic and rectal exams after a hysterectomy. This is true, even if the ovaries were removed. Cystocyles and rectocyles could be picked up and a hemocult test could be performed on a stool specimen. I know for sure that this can lead to follow up studies that pick up cancer of the colon prior to symptoms. Dying in the above case was really a relief for all concerned, but it may not have been necessary.

CHAPTER 16

Anxiety, the Panic Button

I suppose it is always best to give credit to those who teach you, especially when what they teach is put to the test and does not come out lacking. Such is the case here, but I just don't recall which teacher gave this good advice.

Before the local hospital opened and while Munford Clinic was still open at night, I received a call to come quickly to the office. A family said they had called George, the mortician, to come get the patient, whom they stated may be dying. They believed that he was certainly quite ill and the family was quite anxious about him.

I reached the clinic before the patient, yet in a few minutes here comes George wheeling in the patient, who was both quite anxious and quite vocal for help. His family was with him, walking quickly to keep up with George as he rolled the stretcher into my exam room. The patient and all his family, as well as George, were in the exam room with me. The family was very panicky, saying things like, "Dr. Vaughan, do something quick, he acts like he is going to die."

At this point, I recalled what a teacher had said during medical school:

You are going to have occasions when the patient and the family members as well, are extremely upset and anxious. They demand something be done quickly. They will express gloom and doom with expressions on their faces of marked anxiety. The tendency in such cases is for you to become excited and anxious as well. You must not do this. In an anxious, excited, something-must-be-done state, it is difficult to make a good sound judgment. If you check the patient's vital signs and they are OK, then relax, take your time, and figure out what is going on. Chances are they are not very sick.

I followed this advise and examined the patient's vital signs and tried to question him with both he and his family getting frustrated because I was not giving him any medication by shot, IV, or whatever. They wanted me to do something. His vital signs were normal and because I didn't know what else to do and also to try and stabilize the situation, I asked the family to wait outside the exam room. To George I said, "George, you stay in here with me." I, as the old saying goes, decided to bite the bullet and put the teacher's advice to work.

I knew the patient well and he knew me. We were on a first name basis. I just sort of shook him a little, looked him right in the eyes and said to him, "Friend, I want you to know that I know nothing is badly wrong with you. You know nothing is badly wrong with you and I think George knows it too. I want to know what's going on here."

He immediately started to cry and said, "Nobody loves me." He was about thirty years old and was having marital problems. The pain and anxiety just got to him. We talked a while and he returned home feeling much better. I surely felt good about what I had been taught and remembered.

CHAPTER 17

Reaching for the Stars

I referred a neighbor of mine to a surgeon for a lump in her breast. A work-up revealed cancer. Radical breast surgery was performed. This was in the late 1950's or early 1960's. Therapy then was not as efficient as now. She received chemotherapy and radiation, but responded poorly to therapy. She had a very malignant type of cancer and she progressively went down hill. There was no hospice then and being terminally ill, she experienced considerable pain. Oral narcotic medication soon became unsatisfactory, so narcotics by injection became necessary. My wife, in addition to being a good friend to this patient, is also a registered nurse. During the course of this patient's illness, Violet was essentially an on-call nurse. Our neighbor would call and Violet would go and attend to any need.

About three months before she died she spent a considerable amount of money having her house carpeted everywhere except in the kitchen, which had linoleum flooring. Violet and I both felt that it was foolish of her to spend money in this manner, which they really could not afford.

The time arrived when, in my medical opinion, only a few days were left before she would succumb to her cancer. Her food and fluid intake was practically none at all. I advised that she be admitted to the hospital for fluid therapy. She consented to go even though she knew she would never return home alive.

At that time, there was no ambulance service in Tipton County except the ambulance of the funeral home. Munford was most fortunate that Munford Funeral Home had George Baddour as its owner, director, and mortician. He was the most available physician's assistant for ambulance service you can ever imagine. Without fail, every time I called for his help, I got it. He came and we placed Ruby in his ambulance for transfer to Tipton County Memorial Hospital. It happens that the headliner, the fabric covering in the top of ambulance, was a very light blue-gray with stars here and there in a pattern. On the way to the hospital, our neighbor, in a manner of a semiconscious state (for she certainly was not in context of reality) began slowly to reach for the stars. She would try to pick them out of the sky, so to speak. I always rode in the ambulance with my patients. This thought entered my mind, *She knows she is going to heaven and is just reaching for the stars.*

She had made arrangements for her funeral, wake, casket, etc.; the whole bit. She had requested that her wake be in her home. Her body was placed near the wall in her living room requiring you to walk the entire length of the room to view her in the casket. As Violet was standing at our front door watching cars go by to that house which was next to ours, she looked at me in a startled way and said, "She had said to me as plain as day, 'Now you know why I had my house carpeted.'"

CHAPTER 18

Delivering Babies

Talk about miracles. What a miracle a new life is! It was always exciting for me to see a newborn infant make its way out of the birth canal. The head and the shoulders are the largest so they move out rather slowly, the rest of the body just seemed to slide out. Breech births were a different story. I suppose all GPs feel more confident in one field of medicine than another. Obstetrics was my field. I was not qualified to do C-sections but I took my hat off to no one when delivery from below was used. I have memories of numerous deliveries, but a few stand out and are worth telling about.

I delivered several sets of twins during my medical career, but only one set that surprised me by being twins. I expected to deliver just one. Mrs. Janet Pinner had told me on the last two or three prenatal visits, "I believe I'm going to have twins." I would take my fetascope and try to find two heart tones, but never did. When she came into the clinic in labor she again said, "I'm going to have twins."

Stubborn me, I just listened for heart tones again and said, "I hear only one. You're just going to have a big baby." In those days ultrasound was not done and I took x-rays only on those that were having some type of problem or if I was unsure of the presenting part. The presenting part is that part of the baby that comes out of the vagina first.

This patient's labor progressed nicely and was cephalic (head) presentation and occiput anterior (face toward rectum). This is exactly the way you wanted them to be. She proceeded to spontaneously deliver this nice baby boy, but uh-oh! It was obvious her abdomen was not going down like they usually do as soon as they deliver. A quick feel of the abdomen and a vaginal exam let me know there was another baby present. This second baby presented on the next contraction in the same position and delivered spontaneously; just picture book perfect. One thing for sure: when the outcome is good, it never makes a patient upset when you think one thing and they think another. Especially, when they end up right. She was right. I was wrong.

Breech deliveries are frank breech (buttocks, the presenting part), single footling, or double footling. I did not fool with the single or double footling. I was afraid the cord might prolapse out the vagina and be compromised so that the baby's life would be jeopardized. If one of my patients came to the clinic in labor with a presentation of a footling type, I just called an OB specialist in Memphis and I would get in the ambulance with my patient and to Memphis we would go. Once again, I was lucky. None of these prolapsed a cord before we reached Memphis and there a C-section would be performed.

Nowadays, the frank breech would have a C-section. I guess back then we just didn't know things might be as bad as they could, for we just followed them like they were cephalic, waited until the buttocks presented out the opening of the vagina, and then carry them to the delivery room. By this time they would be complete (cervix all the way dilated).

With gentle traction the buttocks and legs would deliver without difficulty, then you could rotate a shoulder underneath the pelvic bone, pull down slowly and the presenting shoulder would deliver out the canal. Then the baby was rotated 180 degrees with its back in the forward part of the rotating, the other shoulder would be under the pelvic bone. With just a little tug downward and forward the second shoulder would come out. Then came the anxiety. The biggest part of the baby is the head and unless the head is delivered within eight or ten minutes the baby could be in real trouble. Out of all the breech births I delivered, I only had one that gave me real trouble. This patient's cervix clamped down after the shoulders were delivered or perhaps the cervix was not completely dilated during delivery to this point. The head was hung up inside the lower uterine segment by the cervix. I knew I had to get that baby out. There are forceps called Piper forceps that are used for this scenario. I had never used them, but now I had no choice.

Absolutely, when you have no choice you do what you have to do. I knew what you were supposed to do with them. They were to be inserted inside the cervix on the baby's head and then using a gentle pulling motion, the baby was pulled through the cervix and out the canal. It is relatively easy to cause a tear in the cervix doing this. Bleeding could occur from the tear. However, at this point my main concern was delivering a viable, live infant. With steadily applied traction, this particular baby was delivered successfully. As with most breech deliveries, the baby was a little sluggish, but cried soon and pinked up nicely. I was happy as a lark at that point. You see, in the country, you are the pediatrician as well as the obstetrician. As soon as a baby is delivered, he/she requires attention. The umbilical cord must be clamped and the baby must be made to cry. Then the mother must be taken care of. Nature must know that's the proper thing to do for the mother is not usually ready for the delivery of the afterbirth (placenta) for a short while. If you have ever watched a cow deliver, it is sort of like that.

After the baby was stabilized, I turned my attention to the mother. After the delivery of the placenta, I inspected the cervix by way of retractors. Uh-oh! I had a long tear to contend with, and I could not actually see the bottom of the tear. I had just one nurse helping me, and she could not take care of the baby, do the other things needed, and help me at the same time. She was not scrubbed. I needed another pair of hands. I needed better exposure of the tear. I did what I thought should be done in this situation. The patient's uterus was firm, she was not actively bleeding, and I knew that Memphis and specialists were not far away. I had the nurse call the ambulance, and the mother, baby, and I were then transported to the City of Memphis Hospital.

I let the residents there know what had transpired so far and they took over. She was carried to surgery in the OB department for cervical tear repair. The tear was a long one. Upon retraction of the vaginal wall and by pulling the cervix forward with ring forceps, the tear extended to the first portion of the uterus. Bleeding during repair required a pint of blood, but all ended well. Mother and baby both did well. I would not have been able to repair this in our clinic. I sure was glad I didn't try. Like I said, I've always been lucky. I never had a serious mother problem and never lost a term baby.

In a small town, country practice, you get to know your patients and they know you in situations other than the doctor and patient status. You and your patients have fun together and kid about things. For example, when I would listen to the fetal heartbeat with my fetascope and the heart rate was 140 or above, I'd say, "It's a boy." When the heart rate was 120, I'd say, "It's a girl." I had no real idea what the sex of the baby was but the old timers used to say that a faster heart rate equals a boy.

The patient could agree or disagree. Most of the time she would say, "Are you sure?" This was all before ultrasound was routine and the sex of the baby was able to be determined before birth. Even now, if I was a parent-to-be, I do not believe I would want to know the sex of the child before its birth.

Talk about being fortunate! If you deliver babies long enough, you are bound to have a complication with a mother that has a bad outcome or a baby that for some reason just doesn't make it. Liability insurance was climbing higher and higher for delivering those babies. Lawsuits in Florida caused things to just go haywire. It became apparent to me that deliveries would be a losing proposition for me. I realized that my time plus liability insurance costs would leave nothing for me as profit, even if I got paid for all deliveries. At this point, I was delivering babies because it was such a satisfactory part of my practice anyway. I felt like I did it well and I had a satisfied patient about 99 and 99/100% of the time. I just liked it. I had less time off and worried about vacationing, etc., because Dr. Sid was not delivering on my nights off by this time. I just quit OB. I quit, as they say, while I was ahead of the game, for I had avoided any disasters in this field of medicine.

CHAPTER 19

Bro. C. B. Betts

When our third child, Keith, was born, Bro. Betts came by our clinic to see Violet, our newborn child, and to congratulate me. Keith was born in the clinic where my office was located. Our last three children were born there; Dr. Sid delivered these three.

When I was showing off Keith to Bro. Betts, he looked like any good looking newborn. His appearance was normal in every way, however, he had an abnormal Moro reflex. This is called the startled reflex. When lying on a table on their back, a newborn will, when you hit the table with your fist, suddenly jerk back and forth with his arms and legs a few times. This is the normal. Keith had a prolonged and exaggerated Moro. He had a sort of seizure-like jerking in his extremities, and continued this jerking for a second or two longer than average. This bothered me, for I was unsure of its significance. I told Bro. Betts this and demonstrated this reflex on Keith so he could see and understand what I was talking about.

After Keith stopped the jerking, Bro. Betts said, "Hugh, do you mind if we have a little prayer about this?"

I said, "Certainly not." I had not heard Bro. Betts pray. I have heard innumerable prayers, before and after this one, but none compare with the manner in which he prayed. He prayed in his normal quiet voice and it was as if he were talking to a friend. The exact words escape me, but it went not unlike this:

> Lord, Dr. Vaughan and I are here with his newborn son. We don't know what's going on here. Dr. Vaughan is concerned. He says his son has a reflex that is not normal to him and that he is not sure of its significance. We don't know whether it is significant or not, but we just wanted to let you know that we are somewhat anxious about it. We are hopeful it will not be a sign of anything serious. Dr. Vaughan and I are grateful to you for this new son and for all thy blessings. Amen.

Unbelievable! There was no hint of wanting a healing miracle; no hint of fancy words such as beseech. He spoke in a tone no louder than his normal talking voice, maybe even not that loud. It was like he was talking to a neighbor at the fence on his property line. It was like he was telling him about Keith and me. He practiced the presence of God. He was talking to a friend.

Keith is now a full colonel in the Army. He is a dermatologist and chief of the dermatology department at Madigan Hospital at Fort Lewis near Seattle, Washington. He has a very minimal (not noticeable) residual of a polyneuritis in which the cause is unknown. His work up as a child was done at St. Jude Hospital in Memphis, Tennessee. His condition certainly ended up not serious.

CHAPTER 20

Prayer

I know that to what extent people believe in prayer will vary from individual to individual. I believe that just about every doctor living that does clinical practice has had the occasion to seek and use prayer as a helper in his or her practice.

There were two religious groups in our little town of Munford that practiced praying over the patient when one of theirs became sick. It was not uncommon for me to make a house call on a patient, and then when I would arrive at the home, go in, and be told the patient was in the bedroom. I would head to the bedroom, and as I would try to approach the patient, I would have to say, "Excuse me," as I parted folks that were there praying over the patient. It never disturbed me that they were there. I did often wonder just how much healing was expected from this practice. *Did they truly expect miraculous healing to occur, or did they feel like accepting things they could not change would come more easily?* I never asked them.

The two groups that practiced this were the Nazarene and the Assembly of God. I was fortunate to have great friends in churches of all denominations. Dr. Sid was a Presbyterian; I was a Methodist for most of my life.

I know absolutely that it is most comforting and gives you a sense of peacefulness to know that you are being prayed for. I know this because I used to get a phone call at least two or three times a week from this dear lady, Mrs. Della Sawyer. She would just say that she wanted me to know that, "I pray for you every day." She was old enough to be my mother. She and her daughter, Mrs. Pansy Billings had been patients of mine for years. They seemed to like me quite well.

After Mrs. Sawyer died, I missed being called and told, "I pray for you every day."

CHAPTER 21

The "Not so Tough" Nut

One of my most memorable patients was a man in his late sixties, who was what many considered to be a tough nut. He was loud mouthed, gruff, and appeared to be quite heartless. Physically, he was a big man with strong arms and talked with an authoritative voice. He was not the type of guy with whom you would want to pick a fight. He seemed to enjoy being cruel to animals, especially dogs. He would knock a dog in the head and throw him into an old cistern on his property. It was rumored that he filled the cistern with dead animals. He would talk boastfully about his exploits in cruelty.

There was just a mean look about him at times, and that, along with his physique, made him appear to be, "King of the Block." He bragged about being boss at home and boasted that his wife did as she was told.

Another married man who was present when this boast was made, was heard to say, "You had better watch the married man who says he is boss at home for he will lie about other things as well."

The above described man was not the type you would expect to pray. I seriously doubt that this man had ever prayed in public.

Why would he ever need God? He appeared perfectly capable of running and controlling his own life without interference from anyone.

Early one morning, " Mr. Smith" phoned me at home, sounding obviously ill and experiencing what, I am sure, he thought were life-threatening symptoms. With extreme urgency in his voice, he whispered, "Can you come and see me right away? I'm real sick. I don't know whether or not I'm going to make it." I went by the office to pick up my medical bag around six o'clock in the morning and to his house I went. When I arrived at the house and knocked on this particular door he had instructed me to use, no one answered.

I thought that maybe he was terribly ill, so I just entered and walked into the bedroom. The sight that greeted me could have knocked me over with a feather. This mean, tough, old, dog-killing man was on his knees at the side of his bed, leaning on the bed with his elbows, and in his normal voice was praying loud and clear, "Now I lay me down to sleep, I pray the Lord my soul to keep."

My eyes moistened with tears. I thought, *This is probably the only prayer he knows to say.* It was like he had reverted to his childhood memories. It was quite a touching moment. He had suddenly become God conscious and needed the help available via prayer. He wanted God, "My soul to take." His condition was minor and he lived many more years. I never looked at Mr. Smith in quite the same way as previously, and I believe that this event transformed him into a much more mellow man.

CHAPTER 22

The Faith Question

One of my good friends, a cattle man who knew how to buy and sell cattle with the best of them, and his minister's wife caught me just as I was leaving the office one day. This cattle man helped me every way he could in my cattle work. I could borrow his cattle truck anytime. He never charged me. He would haul my cattle to the market. He would just help me in anyway he could. He was a member of the Assembly of God church. The minister's wife was one of the best friends Violet and I ever had. Her husband was a great minister and they both could sing so well that they should have been on TV.

This cattle guy got right to the point. He said, "Bro. and Mrs. Prichard and I are going to Memphis tomorrow night to see Oral Roberts. We want you to go with us." They knew I was a minister's son.

I replied, "I wouldn't go across the street to see Oral Roberts."

This cattle guy looked perplexed. He said, "I can't believe you said that. You are a minister's son. Don't you have any faith?" Brother Roberts, at that time, was having tent meetings with the laying on of hands and healing. Folks would come to the altar and tell their tale of sickness or affliction. Then Oral Roberts would pray, lay hands on them, and say, "Heal!" That sort of thing. I never have been a believer in miracle healing of this kind. In my own mind, I thought if Oral was really an instrument of healing in this manner, he would have to get on a plane or helicopter just to rest and sleep. He would be surrounded by sick people beyond imagination.

I said all of that to say this. This cattle guy was named C.D. Demery and called B-Jack. I told this story to everyone, sometimes in front of him. He would just smile. I said to B-Jack, "B-Jack, you have a glass eye (which he did). You go see Oral Roberts and get you a new eye and come back and let me see it. Then maybe I'll go see Oral Roberts." He looked like he had, as the saying goes, been hit in the face with a wet towel. He and Mrs. Pritchard ceased to try to convince me to go see Oral Roberts. B-Jack never mentioned whether he thought he could get a new eye or not, but I got the impression he would not expect to get one. I wondered, *B-Jack, don't you have any faith?*

I am still, years later, of the same persuasion that miracle healing in this manner does not occur. Surely, I would have known someone who personally knew an individual with an unquestionable malady that was healed on the spot. Not so.

Oral Roberts is like my dad was, a Methodist minister. He is also a remarkable TV personality that can quote scripture almost without equal. He was a great fund raiser for himself, his school, and a church where he was preaching if his talent was needed. Oral Roberts is whatever you want to call him. To some, he would be a religious giant; to others he may seem a religious fanatic, an egomaniac, a sincere man, a man with charisma, or perhaps an international star in the religious field. He was one of those celebrities that prompted strong opinions one way or the other in people.

I had three children graduate from Oral Roberts University many years after the B-Jack thing. If I write another book, I'll let you know just how great a school I think he had. This book is about things that happened to me because I was fortunate enough to practice in a small town, about some patient happenings and diagnoses, and about medicine and me.

As to faith, each has his own.

CHAPTER 23

Subluxation of an Elbow

One of my classmates and best friends was an anesthesiologist. He was best man in my wedding and I was in his. We talked medicine and what we did in our field. I mentioned that I only treated fractures of the wrist area if there was minimal displacement. (I tried to stay within fifteen degrees of displacement.) I did not cast those that required anesthesia, either general or local. He said to me one day, "Hugh, you ought to use local. It is really quite easy."

I replied that I didn't like injecting into the hematoma (the swollen, bloody area) of a fracture. I thought this might be a good place to get an infection despite using surgical technique of scrubbing, etc.

Anyway, he said to me, "You can deaden the whole arm easily by feeling the axillary artery (artery in the armpit) and injecting 5 cc's of carbocaine beside and beneath it from both sides. Then just give it about twenty minutes to take affect."

A few months later, a young girl came to the office with a very painful and distorted looking elbow. I had films made expecting to see a fracture but to my surprise, I could see no broken bone at all, just an elbow out of place. The humerus and ulna were not together as they should be. Usually, dislocation, once the pain is relieved, reduces quite easily. It dawned on me what Horace had told me about deadening the arm. I, for reasons I'll never know, decided to try it. I injected 5 cc of carbocaine near each side of the axillary artery, and behind it.

This just happened to be an election day, and it was already three o'clock in the afternoon when I realized I had not yet voted. Since I had twenty to thirty minutes to wait for the anesthetic to take affect and there would probably not be a line at the polls this time of day, I just hopped into my car and headed to vote. I had asked Dr. Sid to keep an eye on my young patient. Sure enough, there was no line. I voted then at Flatwood, which was just a few miles from the office. When I returned to the office and checked on the young girl she was all smiles. No pain, but she still had a distorted elbow. I put traction on the forearm with one hand while holding the arm with the other. I pulled in a circle in the direction of the dislocation and toward a correct position. Immediately I felt a "snap" and the elbow appeared normal. She smiled and immediately said, "Thank you." This just made my day.

I rechecked her elbow by x-ray and it appeared perfectly normal. I decided to put her arm in a sling and have her keep it there and to return in a couple of days. I was concerned about a possible tear of the joint capsule. Her elbow moved about normally after it was reduced. I had her wait in the clinic until all anesthesia had worn off. Vascular and nerve function appeared normal. Two days later she was feeling fine except with some discomfort at the elbow, and it was quite swollen. The swelling was much more than I would have expected. I wondered why her elbow was this swollen.

Since I did not really know, I decided to call an orthopedic doctor whom I had used frequently, Dr. Dodge. I called him and told him the story regarding this little girl. She was eight or nine years old. He said, "Hugh, I doubt the elbow was dislocated.

You don't see that in people. A fracture, yes, but a dislocation would be rare."

I replied that I thought it was a dislocation and that I was sending the girl and her x-rays to him for evaluation of the swelling, which just did not suit me. I sent her immediately from my office to his, which was located in Memphis.

Dr. Dodge called in about two hours and said, "Hugh, you were right. Her elbow was dislocated; however, it is in normal position now. With that much dislocation, this amount of swelling would be expected." He advised active and passive exercise and said time should take care of things. It did and this girl did great with no further elbow problems.

For reasons of which I am not sure, I never used local anesthesia on an arm again. I just think the uncertainty of things and lack of experience here told me to just stay away from this sort of thing. "Do anything you want to, but make sure you feel comfortable about it" became my motto. So I would pass from now on and send this sort of case to a specialist. I seemed always to be lucky in what I did and I sure did not want to press that luck. The tonsil, adenoid bit is a good example. It is the next story.

CHAPTER 24

Tonsillectomy and Adenoidectomy

During internship, I spent six weeks at an ear, eye, nose and throat hospital. It was a part of Methodist Hospital but located several blocks from the main hospital. There I assisted in surgery or watched whatever was going on, as well as doing histories and physicals.

I had watched many tonsillectomies. Some done with a wire loop called a snare and some done with a tonsilartome. I liked the snare best because you could see what you were doing much better. The tonsilartome was used by feel and to me seemed like doing it blind. Anyway, these tonsillectomies were done under local anesthesia and general anesthesia with "drops ether" being used on kids. I thought to myself, *I can do tonsillectomies either locally or with anesthesia and if I do, I'll use the snare.*

Adenoidectomies were all done then with an adenotome. It was inserted into the nasopharynx (above and beyond the soft palate). You inserted it with it open so that when you placed it against the back part of the nasopharynx, you would be over the adenoid tissue and then you could pressure the cutting blade closed and it would clip out the adenoids and hold it in its basket. This was done blind but did not seem bad to me because there wasn't anything that vital where you placed the instrument and you would not be cutting anything that serious if you were off target a little.

I decided soon after starting practice to do some tonsillectomies with local anesthesia and did so without any complications. I always sweated a little when tying off bleeding vessels. Getting down into the throat, mopping blood, and using longer instruments made it frustrating at times. I had such good outcome with this approach I decided to do some kids.

There was a great nurse anesthetist in town by the name of Helen Deneka. She gave anesthesia for a urological group in Memphis, but did not work on Saturday for them. I talked to her about dropping ether for me on some kids if I wanted to do tonsillectomies. She agreed, so we just started doing tonsillectomies on children. This was same day surgery stuff. The Munford clinic, my office at that time, was functioning also as a small town hospital that had all of eight beds. This is where I would do the tonsillectomies. I don't recall the exact date that Tipton County Hospital opened in nearby Covington, Tennessee; but it was in the sixties and after it opened, the Munford Clinic's hospital function ended.

One of my friends asked me to do a tonsillectomy and adenoidectomy on their son. I said OK even though I had never done an adenoidectomy. This young man was about eleven years old. The administrator of the hospital was a nurse anesthetist and she gave the anesthesia. The tonsillectomy went without a hitch. The adenoidectomy was different. I used the adenotome as I thought I should and probably did a fair job, but he kept oozing blood. I held pressure via gauze sponge (blindly, so to speak). Then after a few minutes, I would release the pressure and wait. Several times I thought it had stopped, but then the oozing of darkish red venous blood would resume. This happened repeatedly and I was getting frustrated and nervous; wondering just what I would have to do to stop the bleeding.

I knew I would have to pack his nasopharynx with gauze and have him go to his room with this packing there, tied to a string that came out his mouth and nose in a loop. I also knew that I would have to go out there and tell his parents that the bleeding was not controlled and I had to leave in a packing to control the oozing of blood. The packing would have to stay there for a while, then we would take it out and see what happened. If the bleeding resumed, then he would have to be repacked. This was terribly frustrating for me because I was thinking: *I'd hate to be a parent and be told this.* I would wonder why and you see, I did not know why this was occurring for sure. I was about ready to pack his nasopharynx and take him out this way when suddenly a miracle happened.

The general anesthesia was wearing off and as he began to wake up, he started to vomit, The anesthetist dropped the head part of the table down so that the patient didn't aspirate the gastric secretions. These secretions came out his nose as well as his mouth. No one was ever luckier than me. The acid secretions from the stomach cauterized the oozing small veins and capillaries and all bleeding stopped. He was carried back to the room with no packing and could not have done better.

As for me, I said to myself, *This is enough of this mess!* I quit doing tonsillectomies and adenoidectomies (my first and last adenoidectomy), never to do either again. It seemed I always stopped doing certain things before I had any real problems. The anxiety this case caused me was far too much to suit me. I just didn't get paid enough doing this to make me continue to do either. The fee a general practitioner charged had to be much less than a specialist's fee. I doubt nowadays days any GP would do a tonsillectomy and adenoidectomy. Liability insurance would be increased and the possibility of a lawsuit if some complication occurred would be a likely occurrence. By the way, I never had a lawsuit brought against me. You see, I have been lucky all my life. My daughter, Shelley, says, "Dad, you have been blessed."

CHAPTER 25

Persistent Posterior

The delivery of babies in general practice was one of the easiest things to do and also one of the hardest. It was one of the most difficult when it was associated with complications or the potential for a serious outcome for the newborn and/or mother. It causes anxiety beyond comprehension unless you have experienced it yourself.

Such a case was one in which a prima gravida (first baby) patient labored for an extended period. It suggested that the baby was turned face up toward the pubic symphysis rather than face down toward the rectum. The normal delivery is called occiput anterior, which means the face is toward the rectum, and the occipital bone is toward the symphysis. Head position is given in respect to where the occipital bone is located in the mother's pelvis. During normal delivery, the baby's head progresses through the birth canal, and after the head comes underneath the pubic symphysis, it extends, allowing delivery to be accomplished without too much difficulty. If the face is up, the birth canal is such that head extension is not possible and C-section may be required for delivery.

If labor continues for an abnormally long time, it suggests that the head may be turned wrong. If you determine the face is toward the symphysis and the occipital bone is toward the rectum it is called occiput posterior. If labor continues and no progress is made it is called persistent posterior. You may not be able to deliver the baby via the vagina without rotating the baby's head to a occiput anterior position.

After this patient became complete (the cervix open all the way, as it becomes prior to delivery) and uterine contractions had moved the baby down the birth canal to a point called O station, it is about here that you can, by pelvic exam, tell in most all cases what position the baby is in regarding occipital position. I always felt for an ear. By sliding your fore and middle fingers around the head you can feel an ear. Then it is relatively easy to determine the back of the ear from the front. You see, your fingers slides easily from front to back over the ear cartilage. While approaching from back to front, your fingers hit the back of the ear and it is like hitting a curb. You may feel the ear cartilage between your two fingers. There is nothing to grab between your fingers when approaching from the front. Anyway, I could tell the occiput was posterior and the patient would probably not be able to have her baby vaginally without rotation.

I never did like to do things, what I called, *blind.* The standard maneuver for rotating a baby, required you put forceps on the baby's head as if it were in the normal anterior position, then push the baby back up the canal into the uterus and rotate the forceps 180 degrees. Then, with traction on the forceps, pull the head down and forward into the birth canal. You then remove the forceps, for the baby is now in the right position for delivery. You reinsert the forceps on the baby's head, and by traction accomplish a normal occipital anterior forceps delivery. I preferred to rotate the baby head, by hand, to a transverse position. That is, by use of my hand I would rotate the head so that the occipital bone was facing the right or left side of the vagina. I could apply the forceps to the baby's head in the transverse position without difficulty, then rotate the head, with the forceps, to the anterior position, then deliver the baby in a normal low forceps manner.

I rotated the head to the transverse position by hand, then with forceps to the anterior position and began to try to deliver the baby. I was having to apply too much pressure on my pull to suit me. I thought, *Maybe I have the position wrong. I'll remove the forceps and recheck the baby's position in the birth canal.* Just as I removed the forceps, one blade slipped from my hand and fell to the floor. I told my nurse to boil the forceps for five minutes to sterilize them, since these were my favorite set of forceps. We would just have to wait for them to be re-sterilized.

I was just standing there waiting, when I noticed the sheet draped over the patient's chest, was pulsating at a rapid rate. For some reason the patient had developed a fast heart rate of 180 beats per minute. It was a regular rhythm, so this meant it was probably a fast rate secondary to a firing from the atrium. I began to get anxious and to sweat a little.

I broke my scrub and checked the heart rate and was confident this was a rate I could correct by stimulating the carotid sinus that is in the patient's neck. I did this, and sure enough, she converted to a normal rhythm. By this time, my anxiety for the patient and the baby was quite high. I was not absolutely sure why this had happened nor was I absolutely sure why the pressure pull was more than normal. I was sweating more than I wanted. By now I was almost wringing wet.

The thought of problems with a baby, or baby and mother, was getting to me. I had not previously had serious problems with either that caused me nearly the anxiety this case was producing. I decided that dropping the forceps and the fast heart rate was like an omen. I just should take her to Memphis for delivery. I thought an OB-GYN man was better suited for this case than I was. I phoned an OB-GYN doctor in Memphis, told him about my problem and said, "I'm heading your way with this patient."

The mother remained stable and the baby's heart tones were stable also. The patient continued to have pain, but made no appreciable progress over the hour it took us to get to Baptist Hospital in Memphis. This meant to me the baby had converted back to occiput posterior. After we arrived, the patient was taken immediately to the delivery room. The doctor, who was a good friend, said, "Hugh, why don't you scrub with me and we'll see what is going on here?" I was glad to, for I wanted to know for sure, and it would give me a learning opportunity.

After the patient was prepared for delivery, draped with sterile sheets, etc., the doctor examined her vaginally and said, "Hugh, you are right. It's posterior. We'll just rotate it and deliver." He applied the forceps, pushed the baby back up into the uterus, rotated the head 180 degrees, and pulled forward and downward to re-engage the head. He started to remove the forceps to reapply them in the anterior position. He could not get the forceps out. He began to sweat. After several attempts he was able to remove one blade but not the other. He was sweating profusely. I on the other hand, was dry as a chip. You see, now the responsible party was him, not me. Folks, I'm here to tell you, it makes a big difference. He could not remove one blade comfortably so he decided to reinsert the other blade with the blades being in the upside down manner. He felt it better to deliver her with the baby in the normal position with the blades upside down.

Because delivery of the first child is accomplished easier with an episiotomy (an incision to widen the vaginal opening that usually prevents a tearing of the vaginal opening) he said, "I'm going to do a left and right medio-lateral episiotomy so we will have plenty of room for delivery with the forceps." He did this and delivered the baby without too much pressure pull. He was wringing wet with perspiration now. I was still dry. The baby and mother were fine and both did well without any problems. After he delivered the baby, which was over eight pounds, he asked, "Hugh, do you want to repair the episiotomies?"

I said, "Sure." I knew he was exhausted. This type of anxiety just whips you down quickly. This difficult case for me had become his difficult case. He had never delivered a baby with the forceps in this manner before. He told me so. I don't think he said whether or not he had heard of it before.

Anyway, you have no idea of the relief you have when all ends well. I was most fortunate in my practice regarding deliveries. I had a few babies that were born with abnormalities that required I send them to pediatricians and or pediatric surgeons, though I never had a serious complication with a mother nor did I ever lose a term baby.

CHAPTER 26

Marriage Advice

As one of my duties while interning, I had to start intravenous solutions. The intern on medicine started IVs on medical patients. The surgery interns started IVs on surgery patients, etc. I had good luck in hitting veins, in fact, better luck than most other interns. I should have been better for I worked in the lab two years before interning.

On the third east wing of Methodist Hospital, there was a lady hospitalized who was terminally ill from cirrhosis of the liver secondary to alcoholism. She was as yellow as a pumpkin generally, and her brown eyes appeared to be surrounded by a deep yellow wash. The whites of her eyes were most yellow. She required constant IVs. In those days, you did not have the IV catheters that you have now that are left in for several days. You started a new IV with each new bottle of solution. You had to use a new steel needle each time. The needle stayed in that vein just for that IV. I had good luck in getting into her veins. After I rotated off her service, she asked the floor nurses to page me to start her solutions. She said that I was able to start them better than the other interns.

This lady seemed to really like me. She bought me a new pair of white shoes to thank me for starting her IVs when I was not on her service. Interns were required to wear white shoes. She said, "Yours are worn out."

During one visit to this thoughtful lady's hospital room, I let her know that I was going to get married soon, as Violet and I had recently become engaged. This patient was the wife of a very wealthy business man. She said, "I want to meet your wife to be. I have some advice to give her on how to have a happy marriage."

I said, "OK." A day or two later, Violet and I made our way to her room. I introduced Violet to her. She asked that we sit down, that she wanted to talk to us.

She began by telling us that we could end up like she was if we let alcohol control our lives. She remarked that when she married she was not a drinker, but as the wife of a prominent business owner, she had to be a part of cocktail affairs often. She stated that after many years of social drinking she had become an alcoholic and that we not let that happen to us. She said that it could. She informed us that she knew things with her were beyond repair and that she knew she had just a very short while to live. Organ transplants were not an option then (1954). Violet and I married September 29, 1954.

After this advice about alcoholism, she turned to Violet and said, "Young lady, I want to tell you how to have a happy and successful marriage. Be a lady in the parlor and a whore in the bedroom." She continued, "If you do this, you will not have many problems."

Violet and I were sort of speechless and our comments to what she told us were minimal. She then offered their cabin on Pickwick Lake as a place for us to use on our honeymoon. We thanked her for her advice. We declined the use of their cabin (a mansion actually) on the lake.

When I would be asked for any advice on marriage during premarital exams or at other times, I would get around to telling them what this lady said to Violet and me. Our fiftieth wedding anniversary will be next year.

CHAPTER 27

Lawyers and Lawsuits

L awsuits against physicians, hospitals, nursing homes, and care providers of all sorts are currently rampant. Attorneys advertise, especially about auto accidents, to sue for disabilities, hurt, injuries, or whatever. You are told you deserve compensation for these injuries. If you receive no benefit, you pay nothing. How sad. If a person thinks they have a case, then they should pay their attorney whether they win the case or not. It appears attorneys will convince their clients that they are due compensation. Suit sums are out of this world. Awards of millions are not uncommon, and in the billions for class action suits. I wonder if attorneys investigate all that are in class action suits to know if they really do have symptoms or residuals of negligence on someone's part. I doubt it.

I have never been sued.

I have given several depositions. This would occur when I had seen the patient that was suing at some time or other between the time of injury (whether auto, physician, hospital, or whatever) and before the lawsuit is filed and goes to court. Apparently, the client has to tell what doctors they have seen since the injury occurred. In all, except one, I recall that the patient was not seen at our clinic for symptoms related to a previous injury. Their complaint would be sore throat, chest cold, ear ache, or similar unrelated symptom. The lawsuit symptom or residual would not have been mentioned.

I have a nephew by marriage who is an attorney. He knows that I feel attorneys will make up symptoms for their clients to use in an effort to get a settlement. Those documents that I have seen regarding symptoms will have headache, neck pain, dizziness, anxiety, depression, insomnia, plus many other symptoms that no doctor in the world could review and have any idea what injury occurred to the client. There could be no way you could document a medical cause for all the symptoms and relate them to a specific injury.

An expert witness can usually be found to say yes or no to whatever you wish. Certainly, in those cases I know about, the plaintiff has an expert witness testifying one way and the defense has an expert witness testifying another. The idea is to convince the jury that your client deserves compensation. This compensation nearly always goes beyond medical cost, time off, hospital bill, and attorney fee. Most physician lawsuits are settled out of court because the attorneys will get together and decide on a settlement where the doctor will pay, say fifty thousand dollars and sign a document that states he was not negligent. I never understood this. If there is no negligence then why should he pay? The doctor's attorney most often advises this. He says that it will be cheaper than going to court. The insurance companies play a part in this also, for they know where juries have awarded clients huge sums, when in reality, they deserved nothing.

This lets you know my thoughts about lawsuits in general. This prepares you for the lawyer stories I shall tell.

CHAPTER 28

The Randolph Case

While at home for lunch, I was called and told that I was needed at Randolph where road work was being done, that a man had been run over by heavy equipment and they thought he was dead. I was advised to use the back road for it had been raining a couple of days and the road they were working on might not be passable. I was told to take the road that came out at Mrs. Lela Barton's house. The accident had occurred near her house which faced the road that was under repair.

Violet went with me as she often did on calls. Arriving at Mrs. Barton's house, I only had to walk about a hundred yards to reach the body. For sure, he was dead. His chest was crepitus. His ribs were so shattered you could feel multiple fractures. His large intestine protruded from his rectum. His abdominal wall was lacerated just prior to the pelvic bones so that internal organs were visible. He had been run over by this large wheel on this enormous dirt moving machine. The wheel must have been eight feet tall and two feet wide. It was lunch time. The machine was empty of dirt. The men were riding on the machine, heading to the area where their cars were parked, to eat.

This machine had mud on the wheels and the small fender in front of the front wheel. The victim was standing on this fender and the driver of this machine was heading it toward their cars, apparently, rather rapidly. The roughness of the road, plus the emptiness of the machine made the man bounce up and down on this muddy fender. During one of the bounces, he apparently slipped off the machine and landed directly in front of one of these enormous wheels. There was no way the driver could have stopped before the victim was run over. It had run over him with such weight as to crush him flat, so to speak. Instant death.

Now, the workman's compensation insurance company was not wanting to pay full benefit to his widow for death due to an accident at work. The company was wanting to say he died of a heart attack and fell off the machine, and that he just happened to fall beneath the wheel. I had to testify at the trial.

The insurance company's lawyer questioned me. He asked, "Do you know Dr. William Tribby, the pathologist at Methodist Hospital in Memphis, Tennessee?"

I said, "Yes."

He said, "Dr. Tribby said he might have died of a stroke, ruptured aneurysm, or of a heart attack; that one of these usually caused death in a supposedly healthy person. Do you agree?"

I immediately said, "Dr. Tribby was not told the history of this case. This man was standing on a small fender that was muddy and wet on a bouncy machine, and he slipped off this fender and fell directly in front of one of the wheels of this heavy machine. He was crushed to death. What Dr. Tribby said would apply to a person found dead in bed or who suddenly died sitting in a chair. These reasons would apply in a situation where there were no signs of injury."

I actually told the judge (no jury at this trial) that to say this man died of a heart attack, stroke, or ruptured aneurysm would be like saying, 'if I took a shotgun, and unbeknownst to you, pointed it at your head, pulled the trigger, and blew your head off, that you didn't die from the gunshot wound. You died of a heart attack, stroke, or ruptured aneurysm, and that you did this between the time I pulled the trigger and the time it took the bullets to hit your head.' I mentioned that the history was the major key to determining the cause of death.

The widow received full compensation.

CHAPTER 29

Power of Attorney

This lawyer case is one that I cannot see how any attorney that was honest would have taken in the first place. He had to know what he was asking Dr. Sid and me to do was wrong and would make us sign our names as medical authorities to a complete lie. I have to assume that because he came with some of the family involved, that we would not question anything, just sign our names to a document requested by the daughter of the man with her and the attorney. The attorney, the father, and the daughter were all sitting in Dr. Sid's office.

Dr. Sid trusted everyone. He had been told by the attorney that this man and his daughter would like for him to sign these papers. Dr. Sid assumed it would be proper under the circumstance, for this man and his daughter were with the attorney. Dr. Sid signed the document. The attorney told Dr. Sid that I needed to sign the documents also, that he needed two doctor's signatures.

Dr. Sid came to my office and said, "Hugh, there is an attorney in my office with So-and-so and her dad. They need you to sign a document for them."

I said, "OK." I went into Dr. Sid's office. The attorney put the documents on Dr. Sid's desk in front of the chair so I might sit and sign. He turned to the page I was to sign. I don't know why for sure, but as I started to sit, I said very casually, "What am I signing my name to?" Normally, if Dr. Sid said I needed to sign something I just signed it.

The attorney said I would be signing that Mr. So-and-so was giving his daughter the right to manage his affairs, take care of his money, his property etc. I thought, something must be wrong here so I decided to read the document. It, for all practical purposes, said that I was affirming that Mr. So-and-so was of sound mind and had all his faculties, and that he was willingly doing this. I was astounded. I knew he was not of sound mine and certainly did not have all his mental faculties. He had had Alzheimer's disease for several years. I doubt he even knew who I was and am not sure he even knew who his daughter was. I also knew she was not the only sibling. I turned to Mr. So-and-so and said, " Mr. So-and-so, why are you here today?"

He said, "I don't know."

It became obvious he was not aware of what was going on. I stepped into the hall, found Dr. Sid and asked him if he knew what he had signed. He said, "No, I assumed it was all right with her asking me to sign it with her attorney being there." You cannot imagine how Dr. Sid looked when I told him what he had signed. We went into his office. His name was whited off the document. The red faced daughter, her attorney, and her father left. To this day, she has never mentioned this to me. We are good casual friends. Does money mean this much to folks? Does honesty matter to attorneys?

CHAPTER 30

Bart Threatened to be Sued

I had the occasion to discuss with a patient a situation that had occurred. He came to see me because he had inadvertently run over and killed a lady's dog that ran into the road and ended up in front of his pickup as he was driving down the road. He said he almost wrecked it trying to miss the dog. He stopped and went to the lady's house and told her about the accident. He told her he was quite sorry it happened. In a few days, this lady called him and told him she was going to sue him for killing her dog. He said, "Doc, what am I going to do? I need some pills. This is getting to me. I have trouble sleeping. I can't forget about it. What will I do if she sues?"

I said rather quickly, "Bart, you call her up and tell her to go ahead and sue. Tell her you will just counter sue. Tell her that you can't sleep, can't eat, can't think about anything else, that you hated running over her dog and killing it. Tell her you love animals and that it's her fault it happened, that she should have kept her dog up, chained or whatever, so that it could not run into a public road. Let her know you almost wrecked the pickup because of her dog. Tell her its all her fault.

I gave him nothing. When I saw him a few weeks later at his business I said, "Bart, what ever happened about that dog bit?"

He said, "Nothing, man. I did what you said. I called her and told her I would counter sue like you said, and I haven't heard another word from her."

Perhaps I could have been a lawyer.

CHAPTER 31

A No Fault Accident?

This last attorney story is unique, in my opinion. Lawyers of the plaintiff and the defendant will get together at times and decide on a settlement that they feel will be satisfactory to the one suing and to the one being sued. In this case, I do not know what happened on the front end, but do know what happened later.

This young kid was running and playing as kids will do. He was about seven or eight years old. He was running near the rear of the right side of the school bus as it came from behind the gym where the driver had put gas in it. The driver was going very slowly. This boy slipped and fell just as the bus came by. There was no way for the driver to have known that the boy had slipped just at that moment and that his foot had slid beneath the right rear tire. The bus ran over his foot and caused bony injury and skin problems that required repairing with surgery, braces, and a lengthy rehabilitation. He was expected to have some permanent damage.

The family of this boy decided to sue the driver, the school, and all that would be related to this matter in any way. It was one of those cases where the client's lawyer would have no trouble showing a jury documents proving this boy had been injured, and that he had to have his foot put in a brace, and that he had to have rehabilitation etc. It was a known fact that all this happened.

The family of this boy filed a suit against the Tipton County Department of Public Education and the driver of the bus for two hundred thousand dollars. One hundred seventy-five thousand dollars was to go to the plaintiff, and twenty-five thousand dollars to the mother of the child.

The interesting part of this case is the unknowns. Only in a small country town would you have heard about it at all. People talk in a small town. It was rumored that the family had been offered a tidy sum, but they were not happy with the amount and decided to sue for more. I do not know whether this happened or not.

This I do know. The plaintiff accused the driver of being negligent. The Tipton County Department of Public Education had insurance to the extent of ten thousand dollars but enjoys governmental immunity as to any sum in excess of that figure. The bus driver did not own property of any consequence in their name.

The defendants, in their response to the filed lawsuit, denied negligence on the driver's part. The defendants denied the extent and character of the alleged injury to the boy and demanded strict proof thereof if their rights are to be affected by such allegations. The defendants stated in their response to the filed lawsuit, in essence, that they could show it could not have been the bus driver's fault, that it was more likely the boy's fault.

The attorneys for each side had a decision to make. I don't know their conversations, but know that a decision was made not to go to trial. The plaintiff via their attorney agreed to a settlement of ten thousand dollars. This was the maximum school insurance amount. This was tendered as settlement in full and satisfaction of the lawsuit filed against the school and the driver of the bus. An order to approve a minor's settlement was filed in the circuit court.

It appears, to those of us on the outside looking in, that a jury trial could have resulted in this case despite the governmental immunity. An adverse decision against the defendants and the governmental immunity bit could have resulted in the a larger benefit to the plaintiff. It could have also resulted in the plaintiff receiving nothing whatsoever if the jury decided the bus driver was not at fault. We will never know about this. We just assume that the attorneys for the plaintiff thought the governmental immunity thing would hold up in court and that the driver didn't have enough assets to justify having a trial.

The court ordered this ten thousand dollars be divided in a certain manner, part to the boy, part to his mother, part to their attorneys, and part to the boy's insurance company.

Liability lawsuits are way out of hand in my book. There are times that accidents happen that are unavoidable, and to try and put blame via negligence is absurd.

Lawsuits are interesting. Legal matters are interesting.

CHAPTER 32

My Saddest Day in Practice

Anyone who practices medicine will have days that just seem to not go right. Things just don't seem to click as usual. These days will happen now and then but usually cause no real headache or anxiety. However, my saddest day was much different. It played on my mind for days, months, and even now years later, I still think of it.

This patient was a twenty-four year old female with a cyst near her vaginal opening that had bothered her for a few years. In the past it had become infected, incised, and drained by another physician at least twice. I had seen some relative of hers. They told her to come and see me and that I would fix it for good or something to that effect.

When she came and I examined her, sure enough, there was an uninfected cyst about half the size of a golf ball. She wanted it removed. I told her that I could open it, remove its contents and sew the edges back in a manner that I felt would keep it from forming again. She said that was about what the other doctor had said that had previously opened it. It had been opened twice before. She wanted it out forever. I advised her that I could do that under local anesthesia in my office and would come into the office early one morning and do it. I scheduled elective surgery before office hours so that it did not interfere with my scheduled appointments.

She said, "No, I would prefer to have it done in the hospital so my insurance will pay for it."

I did not really like doing things this way but consented to admit her for a couple of days. At the time it was customary to admit the patient the day before surgery and do lab work and chart work, etc. The surgery was then done on the next day and the patient was kept overnight and then sent home the next day.

She was admitted and this minor surgery was scheduled for the next morning. She was sedated slightly but I talked with her off and on during the fifteen minutes it took me to anesthetize the area and remove the cyst. It peeled out like an onion. No problem at all. I used sutures beneath the skin to close the space where the cyst had been and back to the room she went.

The next morning when I arrived on the floor where her room was located, she was walking up the hallway toward me, smiling like crazy and she said, "I'm ready to go home."

I told her that was fine and that she could go. I had the nurse fix her on the bed so I could glance at my work. She looked as if nothing had been done to her except there was no cyst, just a linear line of laceration repair. She was discharged.

About three hours later, in the office, I received a call from her husband saying that his wife felt funny. She had gotten sick all of a sudden, was sweating and felt fainty. I advised him to take her to the ER and that I would meet them there. I wondered what had happened to her, for things had gone well. I finished with the patient I was examining as quickly as I could and headed toward the hospital. They had arrived just a few minutes before I did. I was met at the ER door by one of the nurses, who said, "Dr. Vaughan, she is dead." And she was. I was stunned. How could I face her husband, her family and explain this sudden demise of someone who just a few hours earlier looked and felt great. It was the most difficult task I ever had as a physician.

When I informed her husband of her death, I requested his permission to get an autopsy so we could know absolutely what had happened. I could not be absolutely sure of what happened any other way. He consented and this was done by a general surgeon, Dr. Billy Shelton McCullough, who did surgery at the hospital. He found what I had suspected but was not absolutely sure about. She had thrown an embolus that was acting as a ball valve in her right ventricle, preventing blood from going to her lungs from the right ventricle. I felt it would be a pulmonary embolism but she never complained of chest pain nor had she coughed up blood. This explained why she was sweaty, fainty, etc., but without pain. The bottom dropped our of her blood pressure. This venous thrombus blocked blood that was suppose to go from her right ventricle to the lungs. She died of lack of oxygenated blood going to her brain and other organs.

I told the family about the clot and how emboli happen and that you just had no way of knowing it would occur. They seemed to understand and they even appeared to feel sorry for me. I'm sure they could tell that I was heart broken. I often thought that if I had refused to admit her, refused to remove the entire cyst, and insisted she allow me to incise and sew the edges of the cyst back, she would be alive today. We will never know for sure. She had four young children.

Can you imagine a sadder day for a physician than this? I certainly can't. The predominant symptom that these patients with emboli have is a fear of impending doom. It is followed by sweating, a faint feeling, and pain in the chest if the embolus goes to the lungs. They have this feeling that something bad is happening to them and it is going to happen quickly. It does. I do not think a doctor living would have anticipated this happening.

CHAPTER 33

"I Shot our Dog"

One of the blessings you receive by practicing in the country is that folks get to know you and you get to know them. This patient story concerns a guy that worked in the ASC office. It is one of those governmental farm programs offices. He helped farmers out any way he could. He helped me out big time on my little seventy acres. His name was "Sheldon."

When I was growing up, I would spend most every summer at my aunt and uncle's farm. I did this from about the third grade until I finished high school. Their names were Richard and Emily Laura Thornley. Aunt Laura was mom's sister. They lived in a neighborhood that was called Flippin. It consisted of a country store, a filling station, and a beer joint. I would go to the field each day with my uncle, who was also as good a friend as I ever had. He taught me how to plow with a one horse plow. I never understood why they called it a one horse plow, for just about everybody used mules rather than horses. I liked farming. You could see at that moment, the results of your labor as you plowed. Uncle Richard made me feel like what I did there was just as important as any type work. I am indebted to them for the things they taught me. I am a gardener now that I am retired.

I had about twenty-four cows at that time but did not have a neck catch that I could use to snap around their heads to hold them to put fly pellets in their ears, vaccinate, hold for veterinarian exam, etc. Anyway, Sheldon knew I had built a pen area on one side of my barn to herd calves and their mothers into to separate out the calves and ship for sale, or whatever; but I had no neck catch that I could use to hold them after their head went though the opening. Just out of the blue he said, "Dr. Vaughan, I'll build you the catch if you'll just buy the lumber and the hardware." Believe me, I did, and had one of the nicest places to move cattle into and with little effort have them caught for whatever purpose I needed. Sheldon was about fifty years old.

His wife, Gertrude, called me and said with much anxiety in her voice, "Dr. Vaughan, can you come to our house right away? I think Sheldon is dead." I said I would and headed that way as soon as I finished with the patient I was seeing. I drove with as much speed as I felt safe driving. I just could not believe he would be dead. He was a specimen of health, a nice size guy with a ready smile and he had had no serious illnesses.

I arrived there probably twenty or twenty five-minutes after the call came. He lived several miles from Munford and the road there was, as they say, as crooked as a snake. Gertrude was standing over him as he lay on the floor. He was obviously without vital signs and had been for probably twenty five or thirty minutes. He showed no response to adrenaline into his heart. I felt that after this length of time CPR would be to no avail and it was not done.

Gertrude told me what had happened. He had Angus cattle on his farm and had had problems with coyotes killing a calf now and then. About two hours before I got there, he had heard his cattle bawling like they do when they are calf anxious. He thought that perhaps coyotes were after a calf. He grabbed his shotgun, loaded it, and headed for the pasture.

Sheldon and Gertrude had a dog that had been with the family a number of years. It was a part of the family, so to speak. This dog was so old and so arthritic that it could hardly walk, but tried to go with Sheldon wherever he went. They felt sorry for their dog but just couldn't have it put to sleep. I'm not sure, but I believe it was also nearly blind. Anyway, their dog was living a miserable life.

On this day, the poor dog followed Sheldon with marked effort. After Sheldon got to the pasture where the cows were, he found no coyotes and I believe he decided to put their dog out of its misery. He returned home, laid the shotgun against the wall and said, "Gertrude, I shot our dog." Then he immediately fell to the floor. This was apparently instant death. He never uttered another word.

We will never know absolutely, but it appears he died of an acute episode that may have been related to his shooting the dog. We know the autonomic nervous system can speed the heart quickly or slow it quickly. The adrenaline burst we get when we are scared puts our heart in action to put out more blood per minute and our blood pressure increases and we are prepared for fight or flight. The other side of the coin is that the autonomic system, via the vagus nerves, which causes lowering of the heart rate and I suppose could cause a momentary stoppage where blood pressure will fall, sweating appear, and fainting follows.

Perhaps Sheldon had a cerebral artery aneurysm or an abdominal aneurysm rupture due to increased adrenaline input. Perhaps he had an acute myocardial infarction (heart attack) with cardiac arrest that just happened at this time. Ventricular fibrillation that persisted could have been the cause of death. Perhaps he had an acute pulmonary embolus from a slowing of the heart beat long enough for a clot to form in his legs or abdominal veins and upon heart beat acceleration, the embolus moved to his lungs causing sudden death. I have no way of knowing just what happened to cause his sudden demise, but I will always believe it was related to an emotional stress crisis that was precipitated by his having to put his beloved dog out if its misery. It appeared as if this killing of the dog just put into motion an emotional stress situation that killed him. This was a most sad day for all that knew Gertrude, Sheldon, and their family.

I signed the death certificate as I recall, "dead on arrival," and noted on the back a short history and said he probably died of (1) cerebral vascular accident (a stroke), (2) myocardial infarction (heart attack), or (3) ruptured aneurysm (blood vessel bursting). Statistically, if someone suddenly dies that has been in apparently good health, it would be caused by one of the three.

CHAPTER 34

Two Years without Dr. Sid

D r. Sid and I were a full time partnership until January 1, 1985, as I recall. We were playing in a doubles tennis tournament at the Woodstock Country Club in October of 1984, and had just finished getting badly stomped. He said, as soon as we got in the car, "I'm sorry I played so badly." He was definitely not himself. He was a complete competitor, a great athlete, but this afternoon he was just not playing his good game. He said, "Hugh, I've been wanting to talk to you. I want to retire at the end of the year."

It's a wonder I did not have a wreck, for driving, after this unexpected news was not on my mind. I did not know what to say. I didn't know how I could handle the clinic by myself, even though it was not a hospital now and had not been since about 1965. We worked hard daily, both of us. What would I do alone? How could I pay him his half of the clinic he owned? How could I survive all by myself? What would I do about our employees? All kinds of questions were running through my mind, and I had no answers.

We decided to think about it and talk about details later. He said that he would prefer not to retire completely, that he'd like to take a couple of months off and go to the island of Efate, where he was during the war. He said it was a paradise place. He said that after his trip he would like to see a maximum of five patients per day and no more than that and that if he didn't want to come in at all, he wouldn't. Now, how in the world would this work? How could we arrive at pay, at expense proportions, etc.? And what about clinic dual ownership? I owned half by now. Office calls were fifteen dollars at that time. We had seven employees. Who would we let go? How much should Sid get? How much rent should I pay him? How much should he pay for his help while seeing his five patients? It seemed so complicated that I was just between the proverbial rock and hard place.

Then, all of a sudden, while I was thinking about it, a possible solution dawned on me that maybe we could do this. Dr. Sid would be paid fifteen dollars for each patient that he saw up to the five. If he saw three patients he would get forty-five dollars; if five, then seventy-five dollars. He would get this in cash whether they paid their bill or not. The fees from any lab work, x-rays or medication which he ordered would take care of his share of the overhead for that day. The fact that he was still using the clinic eliminated the problem of buying his share of the clinic or paying him rent. I would pay all employees, all supply expenses, all utilities, and any other overhead expenses. I would pay Dr. Sid cash for the patients he treated before he left that day. Annette Hanks, our receptionist, did this every day that he worked. The last two employees hired were laid off and they seemed to understand. Dr. Sid said he would work for me when I took vacation and we decided that he would be paid one thousand dollars per week while I was gone. He said this arrangement sounded good to him and so it was decided.

It is unbelievable that we never had a cross word, not even a sarcastic word to each other. People don't understand this and I'm not sure I do either, but for sure, if you didn't get along with Dr. Sid there is not a soul living you could get along with. He is a gentleman of the highest order and a professing Christian without equal. I have never known a better person. I could not have found a better doctor or person to work with by looking all over the world.

I decided to continue taking Wednesdays off, so we just closed the clinic on Wednesdays. This worked like a charm for two years. I had to work a little harder to see the patients that normally saw me as well as Dr. Sid's patients. The people in the small town and the surrounding communities adjusted to this change without much trouble. It soon seemed that there were just about five patients each day that requested to see Dr. Sid. People realized that my time was not as available as it had been. He saw his five and I saw all I could between nine o'clock and noon and between one-thirty and four-thirty in the evening, the new hours that Dr. Sid and I had established by 1985. We had patients at Tipton County Memorial Hospital, so trips there (fifteen miles) were made before and after office hours as required.

The winter of 1987 was especially cold and snowy and the holidays came in such a way that more off time was created. The clinic was closed more days than usual. This is OK with workers generally, but for me it was boring. I do *nothing* very poorly. I remarked to Dr. Sid that time off was bad for your health. He said, "Tell me about it."

I said, "Doctor, if you feel that way you ought to come back to work. I mean full time."

He replied, "I've been intending to talk to you about that. I will be in this afternoon after you close and we will talk."

When he came in that afternoon, the conversation went about like this. I said, "Dr. Sid, I assume you meant you wanted to come back to full time work and if that is what you want, come on. Things will be like they were."

He said, "That's what I'd like and if it's okay, I'll start the first of the month."

I said, "Fine."

Now, this was about the end of the first week in January. On February 1, 1987, he began full time work. New employees were hired and our partnership resumed just as it had been all the years. As Jackie Gleason would say, "How sweet it is!" Things were once again our old normal.

CHAPTER 35

The Attorney's Wife

There is no question that physicians practice defensive medicine now. Lawsuits are frequent and as a result of this, the medical community does not hold attorneys in the highest regard. Trivial lawsuits are settled for a sum of money rather than going to court. This practice is, in my opinion, beyond the ridiculous. I was certainly aware of the possibility that I could be sued but did not dwell on it very much. Anyway, to see an attorney or a member of his family would bring this to mind in case I ever forgot.

Munford was the home of Wally Bard an attorney, but a great guy nonetheless. Wally's office was in Memphis. He was in with a large group of attorneys. As a matter of fact, he was the attorney for Lisa Marie Presley, Elvis' daughter. He was hired to represent Lisa Marie in regard to the estate of her father until she became of age to manage her own affairs. I don't know what constitutes an attorney of renown, but I would say Wally was an attorney of considerable stature.

Wally called me one morning just before I left to go to the office and said he would like for me to come to his home and see his wife, Ruth. He said she was having abdominal discomfort. I told him that I would, but it would be much better if he could bring her into the office. There, I could get a blood count, urinalysis, or any other lab work I felt was indicated. I told him that this lab work was important if, for example, I suspected appendicitis. Also, I could do a more thorough exam in the office. He agreed and brought her into the office.

Ruth's pain was in the lower abdomen and more on the right side, as one might expect with appendicitis. The exact history of the illness escapes me, but it seems she had been having discomfort for a few hours. I had the nurse prepare her for a complete exam and had ordered a blood count, urinalysis, and a pregnancy test because her menstrual history was not exactly normal. This menstrual period was a little late. She did not appear acutely ill and was not febrile.

On physical exam things were pretty normal until I did a pelvic exam. She was spotting a little and in her right adnexa (the area adjacent to her uterus where the tubes and ovaries are located), I could feel a fluctuant mass about the size of a goose egg. I thought that maybe this could be an ovarian cyst or tubal pregnancy. Her pregnancy test was positive and her blood count was not diagnostically helpful. She was very slightly anemic, but this was not particularly uncommon in women. I thought to myself that this had to be a tubal pregnancy that was going to rupture soon. She was spotting and the positive pregnancy test made this the primary diagnosis.

I thought, *I flat don't want it to rupture here in the office and make her an acute surgical emergency.* I sure didn't want her getting shocky, fainty, and all that goes with the internal bleeding that would occur with rupture of an ectopic tubal pregnancy. I advised her that I thought she had a tubal pregnancy and that I would like to start an IV, since she would need one as soon as she got to the hospital anyway. I also told her that I was going to call the EMS ambulance for transportation, and that I was going to call a surgeon to see her as soon as she arrived at the hospital. She was agreeable.

I called both, but to my dismay, I could not get an EMS ambulance. The two that were in the county were both in use and not available. I was told that one would not be available for forty-five minutes to an hour. This did not suit me. I felt her encapsulated pregnancy sac could rupture anytime and the bleeding that would occur could be quite serious. I looked at my nurse and said,

"Joyce, you hold the IV bottle. We are going to Methodist Hospital in my car." I was somewhat anxious and worried about the possibilities. I said a silent prayer. I never wanted bad results on any patient but for sure, an attorney's wife just compounded my anxiety.

I had an older model green Oldsmobile that I had purchased for one of our kids and I happened to be driving it on this day. Joyce and I had Ruth lie down on the back seat with her head on a pillow and Joyce sitting in front of her on the seat edge holding the IV bottle so the saline would drip, keeping the IV open. We told Wally to follow us in his car.

The trip (twenty-four miles) to Methodist north ER was uneventful. We wheeled Ruth into the ER and informed the staff there of the probable diagnosis and that Dr. Jones was to be her doctor. He was notified of her presence. Studies there in the emergency room confirmed my diagnosis of tubal pregnancy and soon thereafter, Ruth was in surgery for removal of her ectopic pregnancy. She did fine. She was actually calmer appearing and acting than I had felt inside the whole time.

Now, some attorneys are still going to sue doctors at the drop of a hat. But I'd bet Wally would just about sue any attorney that even thought about bringing a suit against me. No one could have been more appreciative of my services during this medical problem.

CHAPTER 36

Lincoln Story

Sending patients to counselors was never one of my long suits. If there were psychiatric problems as schizophrenia or clinical depression then I found psychiatric consultation a great help. A situational problem, such as marital difficulty, work frustrations and the like just seemed to me to not be helped by counseling. I just didn't have much confidence in the situational counselor for my experience with them was unsatisfactory. The patients who talked to me about going for counseling were mainly those wanting to see marriage counselors. They generally ended up saying that they did not get help. Two people I recall right off told me the counselor (males) made sexual advances and innuendoes toward them (females) after a few sessions. I wondered if marriage counselors were very useful; were they good or bad?

My story here concerns a Presbyterian minister who came to see me for a medical exam, yet he had a Methodist Hospital form. I said, "Say, you are a Presbyterian preacher, what are you doing with a Methodist Hospital exam form?" He advised me that he was going to take a course at Methodist Hospital on counseling. I told him that I was not a fan of that sort of thing in general. I told him that I had heard a great speaker say that if Abraham Lincoln had been born today under the circumstances of poverty, the kind of house he was born in may not have had a south side, etc. and that the welfare folks and counselors would have taken over his family, lock stock and barrel. The rest of the story would be that you would never have heard of him again.

This minister's visit was about two weeks after the postal worker in Oklahoma City had gone into the post office and murdered several of his co-workers. Those not killed were furnished counselors by the Postal Service. I asked the minister just what these counselors could tell those folks that would make things better. It had always appeared to me that given time, people adjust themselves to situations like this. I felt adjustments to a situation would come out satisfactory by individual adjustment. Psychiatric problem adjustment is a different ball game.

After all of my rambling about Lincoln and the postal workers, he asked, "Just how well did you know Lincoln?" I said that I didn't know him well, but that I had heard Lincoln had a great mother and an even greater step-mother. That these ladies taught him that honesty was a virtue without circumstance and that you were completely honest or you were not honest at all. Abraham Lincoln became known as "Honest Abe." He then asked if I had ever heard of John C. Calhoun. I replied, "Yes, I'm a distant relative of his. My mother was a Calhoun."

This set him back a little but he continued after looking surprised. In Calhoun City of South Carolina or North Carolina, (I don't recall which) there was a woman who worked in an inn there by the name of Hanks. John C. Calhoun would come to the inn on weekends and they would be together. Another guy also came and visited this Hanks woman and she married him. They went West together. When their child was born the people from Calhoun City said that their newborn was John C. Calhoun's child. The Lincoln's named him Abraham.

The minister said this story was handed down from generation to generation and is told as truth but that he personally doubted it.

Now, am I lucky or not? I get to hear this great story just because a Presbyterian minister came for an exam to attend a class on counseling. Visiting with your patients a little outside of their reason for the medical visit was one of my great pleasures of practicing medicine in a small town.

CHAPTER 37

Guardian Angel

Violet always said I had a guardian angel. I think this had its origin after she went on a house call with me to see "Hank Smith's" dad. I don't recall his first name. They were black patient/friends of mine and lived on the bottom land that ran up to the Mississippi River. Their house was on stilts, built on telephone poles. It was a typical type of share croppers house in the bottom. It was narrow and not very big. The living and bedroom areas were in the front of the house and the kitchen and back porch were at the back. You could park a car under the house if you wanted to. Pig pens, a chicken house, and fruit trees took up part of the yard and the rest just became crop fields with no fence.

This bottom land would flood in late winter or spring. It might be several days when you could not get in or out of the house without a boat. We had had a rather large rise in the river level this particular year and the current of the river was quite swift. When flooding occurs, sandy loam soil is deposited over the bottom land as the water recedes after flooding. Areas of the river bank are washed away entirely. At times there will be thirty or forty yards of the bluff bank just swept away and a new river bank is left behind. The bottom road would, by necessity, change because of this.

This particular night that I went on the call to the Smith house, was shortly after there had been flooding. Violet was with me. I had not been over the road since the water had receded. Anyway, it was a very misty, foggy, dark night, so that seeing the road, which was just bottom land that had been traveled over, was hard. The misty fog required windshield wipers. Seeing the road was really tough. The Smith's lived about one and a half or two miles down this road and their house was not far from the river bank. We were driving slowly down the road which wound around the river bank and was very curvy in areas. Suddenly, I just couldn't see the road at all. The fog was quite thick. Things just looked eerie.

I decided to stop, get out, and take a look at things. I got out of the car in the fog so that I could see better. As I walked toward the front of the car I could not have been more surprised. The road had washed away and we were just a few yards from driving right into the river. The water of the river did not come up to the top of the bank. From the top of the bank to the water must have been about ten to twelve feet at that time. It became apparent to me by looking around, that the road I had been driving down had washed away into the river and I could discern new tracks about twenty feet to my left going around the washed out area. The fog had prevented me from seeing this in the car. I backed up and got on the new tracks, taking the new road, slow and easy, which had been made merely by traveling on it. We made it to the Jones' house. I did not return the same way I had come but continued on southward and ended up in Shelby County and to a safer roads.

At the Smith's house, I again encountered the small world phenomenon. After examining the patient, making my impression and disposition, I visited a little, as was customary on house calls. I told Mr. Smith that my granddad had preached at Randolph, a small community about four or five miles from his house, and that he had also preached on Island 35. Island 35 was an island located on the far side of the river from the Jones house. He had to get there by row boat. Mr. Smith could hardly believe he was hearing what I had said. He quickly told me that he remembered my granddad well. He had actually rowed him over to Island 35 on occasion and told me that they had been coon hunting together. I was seeing him in about 1965. My granddad had preached there in 1933. My grandfather was Thomas Ewing Calhoun. He was a Methodist minister.

On the way home, Violet said my guardian angel made me stop the car and get out and look around. Otherwise, we would have just perished in the river. Whether a guardian angel did this or not I don't know, but to have a guardian angel sounds great to me.

CHAPTER 38

Signing the Death Certificates

O ne thing that I know for sure, is that some of your patients are going to die, and if you are the one that sees them to pronounce them dead then you are the one that signs the death certificate. I must be strange, peculiar, or something, for I never did understand that phrase: "pronounce them dead." I never heard a doctor *pronounce* someone dead as, "I pronounce this patient dead." Most, by far, that I as the signer of the death certificate saw were seen in the home or were brought by my house by the funeral home staff in their ambulance. In Tennessee, the body had to be seen by a physician or coroner before the funeral home staff could take the corpse to the funeral home for embalming.

Dr. Sid and I had a sizable number of people from the county to our south, Shelby County, as patients in our practice. If patients died at home there and no doctor or coroner was available to see them in the home, they had to be taken to the Shelby County morgue in the City of Memphis (John Gaston) Hospital. If it were, like ten o'clock at night, the body might not be checked by a doctor, pathologist, or a resident doctor until mid morning the next day. The family would have the extra expense of transportation to and from this hospital, the expense of mortuary storage for a day, as well as knowing that the body could not be prepared for visitation for another day. The body would just be there in the cold morgue.

This was disturbing to some, so Dr. Sid and I would go into Shelby County and see the corpse. We would always do this when asked by the funeral home staff, even if the person was not one of our patients. It was a courtesy thing. The funeral homes we were involved with always helped us anyway they could. The same thing was true in our county, Tipton, except the corpse would be taken to Tipton County (later Baptist) Memorial Hospital. The funeral home staff could transport the body to my house or Dr. Sid's house. We could view and examine the corpse and let the funeral home staff know the person was dead. They could then take the body to the funeral home for embalming and preparation for viewing, etc. They would let us know if coming by our homes was their preference.

In the person's home, I would observe and examine the corpse to make sure there were no signs of life or do the same thing in the ambulance if they brought the body by my house. I found out in early years of practice that you had to be a little careful here. A person that had bad emphysema would go without an audible heart beat for a long time and you would think they had breathed their last breath. Then there would be another gasp. This might happen several times after no heart beat could be heard for an extended period. I have listened and watched until I just knew the end had happened. I would start to get up from a chair to let the family know that it was over and low and behold, there would go another gasp.

So much for generalities of signing the certificate. Now for the story of one I signed. It was either September or October, for cotton picking time was in full bloom. I was called to come see this man that died sitting in his chair at home. He was an Afro-American. He was in his eighties. The family told me that they had been in the field picking cotton and returned home for dinner. (It was lunch time, but we southerners will say dinner for mid day meals and supper for evening meals a lot of the time.) They found him sitting in his chair, "Just like he is now." He was neatly dressed in his overalls and had on a well ironed, neat gray shirt. His head was slumped forward. His arms were stiff with rigor mortis. He had been dead a while. The family said he had felt good and that except for his age he would have been picking cotton with them. They said that he was sitting in the chair when they left the house to pick cotton earlier that morning. When they returned they found him like this.

I always listened for heart tones. I guess I did this for the family's sake. I did this when I knew without doubt I would hear nothing. I unbuckled his overall strap on one side, then unbuttoned his shirt and stuck my stethoscope over his heart area and listened for a few seconds. I heard nothing, of course. I then said, "I'm sorry. What funeral home do you want me to call?" They said the Ford Funeral Home in Memphis, as I recall. Anyway, it was one that Afro-Americans owned. They came and picked the body up. I signed the death certificate in this manner: "Cause of death: dead on arrival. See back." Death certificates have a place for you to write lengthy on the back if you so desire. I wrote on the back: "This elderly man was found by his family sitting slumped in his chair, dead. They had been picking cotton. I believe he died of an acute myocardial infarction, a ruptured aneurysm, or cerebral vascular accident. This is heart attack, a rupture of a major blood vessel, or a stroke." One of these would be the most common cause of death where there is no history of severe illness or injury.

Afro-Americans may not have the funeral for up to several days. It was about four or five days later that my receptionist buzzed my office and informed me that a nice dressed guy was up front wanting to see me. She said he is a reporter. I said, "When I finish with this patient, you may send him back." She did.

He stepped into my office and said he would like to ask me a few questions about the Afro-American that I had seen and pronounced dead of natural causes. I said, "Why?"

He said, "That man was murdered." I could hardly believe my ears. He said, "There will be an article about it in tomorrow's *Commercial Appeal*." (the Memphis, Tennessee paper) Sure enough, there it was. It told how he had been seen by Dr. Hugh Vaughan of Munford. It said I had signed that he died of natural causes. The facts were, after three days the funeral home where the body was, notified the police that this man had been shot in the abdomen with a shotgun. The wound had been stuffed with cotton. His bloody clothes that he was wearing at the time of the shooting were found under the front steps of the house. He had been cleaned up well, dressed neatly and placed in the chair.

I wondered, who in the world, and why in the world, would anyone want to murder as old a man as this. Needless to say, in the future I looked the corpse over pretty good. In a small town, folks let you know what they read in the paper.

I heard from lots of folks.

CHAPTER 39

Discipline

In general medicine you see families with one, two, three, or more siblings and it is interesting to see how well parents are able to instruct their children in behavior and their child's response to instruction.

One parent's instruction often carries more weight than the other. In boys, it seemed to be the dad that carried the most authority. The child appeared to know what would happen if they didn't mind. With girls, the mother was more likely to get good compliance with instructions. In my early years of my practice, spanking by a parent with a switch or belt was a way of enforcing compliance to instruction or command. In later years parents had to deal with the "child abuse" situation. Social workers at school would report parents that whipped their kids.

I feel confident is saying multiple siblings in a family yield children that mind their parents better than a single child family. There are exceptions, of course.

CHAPTER 40

Laceration Discipline

This story about parental discipline concerns a boy about thirteen years of age. He was quite large for his age and had the reputation of being tough. He had sustained a facial laceration very near his left eye. His mother brought him to the office for me to repair this cut. It was about an inch and a half long and a half inch deep. He was placed on the surgery table and cleansing around the area was accomplished. The surgery tray was prepared. I put on my gloves and filled a syringe with carbocaine so that I might deaden the area involved.

I always explained to children what I was I was going to do, that it might sting a little at first, but that it would not be bad at all. I assured them that after I had numbed the area there would be no pain whatsoever, just a touch feeling. Most children permitted local injection without undue movement or fuss. This young boy was different. When I would approach the wound with the syringe, the needle on it was more than he wanted to endure. He would grab my hand quickly. It was like being in a vice. I explained to him that it was necessary that he remain still, that the cut was very near his eye, and if he jerked or moved I might not be able to keep the needle from scraping his eye.

I instructed him again on what we would do and that he was a big boy, that it would hurt practically not at all. As I approached the cut area again with the syringe, it was just like before. He grabbed it. My hand was back in the vice. His mother and I talked with him. She pleaded, "Son, please be still, Dr. Vaughan said it would not hurt much to deaden it."

I tried the third time. He let me get a little closer to the laceration area this time, but again he grabbed my hand. I decided that this scenario would recur each time. I told his mother that she would have to take him to the hospital to get his cut repaired, that he probably would require general anesthesia. You may hold infants or small children relatively easily, but this boy could have beaten me in a fight. He was tough. I took off my gloves, walked out of the surgery room and began to see patients that had been waiting for too long a time. We treated lacerations as emergencies. We would repair them as soon as we finished with the patient we were seeing when they came in.

About twenty minutes later, this boy's dad came in with his son and asked me if I would consider trying again. He said he was sure his son would not give me any trouble. He and I were personal friends. We had bird hunted together. His family and his dad's family were patients of ours. I had even repaired an umbilical hernia on one of his bird dogs just for the fun of it.

Back to the surgery room again. Preparations were repeated, new cleansing, new surgery tray, new draping, new syringe, new gloves, the whole bit. I again let the boy know that it would sting just a little. As I took the syringe and started toward his eye area, his dad said, "Son, you better not grab Dr. Vaughan's hand, if you do you are in trouble." The difference was unbelievable. This boy not only did not grab my hand, he practically did not even bat his eyes. He remained as still as a mouse. Repair was accomplished with no problem at all. He knew his dad was bigger than he was and that he was the authority. I'm sure via experience, he knew who held the high cards. Dad was the authority in this case, and his instructions meant to him: *"I need to do what he says."*

He had been disciplined by his dad before.

CHAPTER 41

School Bus Problem

This second case is similar but under different circumstances. I happened to be chairman of a bus committee that was responsible for two bus routes and the drivers of each bus of a private school. Children were troublesome at times, but the drivers could handle most problems. If they couldn't, they would come to me for help. This one driver, Mr. Bill Melton, a prince of a fellow and an excellent driver, was loved by all the kids. He had one boy that persisted in causing trouble, enough so, that he became exasperated and asked for my assistance.

When he told me the boy's name, I said, "Don't worry, you won't have any more trouble with him." You see, I knew this boy's dad well. He and his family used to live two doors from my office. I knew the father was the authority at his house, and that his son knew it. This dad didn't tolerate one of his children being disrespectful, not minding, and especially, not being courteous to the older generation.

I made it a point to be at the school when the busses arrived the next morning. This was before office hours. When Mr. Melton's bus unloaded, I was at the door waiting for all to disembark. I tapped the boy on the shoulder and told him that we need to talk a few minutes after everyone was off the bus. I don't know for sure, but I think he knew why I was there. I told Mr. Melton to sit tight, that he, this boy, and I needed to talk. After all were out of the bus, this young man and I entered and sat on the front seat. I told this boy that Mr. Melton had informed me that he was having a problem with him. I then told him that I wanted him to know if he continued to cause a problem, that I would take him straight to his dad.

Mr. Melton had no more problems with him.

To let you know what this country doctor did regarding parental discipline, I used my belt. It was always handy. I wish you could know our children. They are grown, married, and some have kids. We never had a problem of serious nature with any one of the five. I believe that each one likes and loves me and their mother. Each one was belted at one time or another. I do not think they believe they were abused.

Discipline, in my opinion, is actually both wanted and needed by children. I believe they desire to know where you stand, whether or not you are consistent, and do you mean what you say. Children need to know that when you instruct them to do this or do that, you mean business, that it is not an imaginary thing that will happen to them if they fail to comply. Parents need to stick to temporarily imposed rules like 'no phone for a week,' 'no car for a week,' 'no friends over for a week,' 'no going out to play until your work is finished,' or whatever. Children need and want to know the ground rules deep down.

Appropriate and consistent discipline is important.

CHAPTER 42

The Right Leg Problem

You do not practice medicine long before you find out that there will be times when a patient must surely have something wrong with them, yet you do not have the slightest clue as to what it is. This happened to me with our first child, Hugh Jr., when he was about fourteen months old.

Violet and I would get up in the morning about the same time. She would get Hugh Jr. up and then fix breakfast. I would be shaving, showering, and getting dressed.

This one morning Violet called me to come to Hugh's bedroom. There was some anxiety in her voice. I rushed to the room where he slept. He was still in his baby bed. He was lying on his stomach crying. Violet said, "He won't stand up. His right leg hurts." She reached over the bed rails to stand him up. He would just flex (draw up) his right leg and begin to cry. I tried. I picked him up under his arms and tried to let him down so he would be standing on his feet. Again, he would raise the right leg and cry. He would not put any weight on his right leg or foot. I could find nothing strange by looking at or by feeling his leg and foot.

I decided to dress quickly, eat a bite, and take him to the clinic for some x-rays. We carried him there and made x-rays.

The multiple view x-rays were all normal to me. I examined him good again, and still no sign of anything abnormal showed up. Repeated tries to get him to stand were in vain. He would cry a minute or two after you laid him down, and then he would seem to be all right.

When a patient is stable and the diagnosis is uncertain, watchful waiting is always in order. I decided to let him lie on one of our clinic beds and let time go by while I saw patients. Every hour I would go in, pick him up, and try to get him to stand and walk for us. No luck whatsoever. This went on until eleven o'clock. Hugh was still symptom free when he was just lying there on the bed. He seemed happy at the attention he was getting. Violet was getting anxious about him. I had no clue. She decided that I didn't know much about kids, especially ours, and that we should take him to see Dr. Whittemore, an orthopedist whose office was in Methodist Hospital in Memphis.

I called Dr. Whittemore and told him the story. He told me to bring him down during lunch and that he would see him first off after he returned from his lunch. I carried Hugh from the parking lot to the office part of Methodist Hospital. I tried to get him to stand. Same results, he would raise his right leg and cry. When we got on the elevator to go to the third floor I tried again. It was in vain.

Violet had Hugh's x-rays. I carried him down the hall to Whit's office. The receptionist knew me and knew we were coming, She said, "Go on back to Dr. Whittemore's office. He is expecting you."

We went into his office. Violet handed him Hugh's x-rays. When Whit was looking at the x-rays I told how repeated efforts to get him to stand were futile. After he reviewed the x-rays, I said, "Let me show you how he does." I turned Hugh around from the way I was holding him, put my hands under his arms, and started to stand him. He let me put him down standing and just walked around the office like nothing had ever happened. I could have paddled him. Flabbergasted is inadequate to describe how Violet and I felt. Whit just grinned. He examined him a little and said that with kids nothing surprises him. He, of course, found nothing.

Violet and I, as the saying goes, tucked our tails and went home. Hugh had no more leg problems.

CHAPTER 43

Drinkers: Uncertanties in Medicine

We have all heard that you never say never in medicine; that there are no absolutes. I can throw a kink in that wheel real quick. I never knew how to treat alcoholics satisfactorily. I seemed to have absolute failure in getting them to stop drinking. I had difficulty getting things in perspective regarding alcoholics.

When I was in medical school, probably the second or third quarter, my dad was visiting me. He needed to go to Methodist Hospital to see a member of his church. A fellow classmate of mine joined us when we left to go to the hospital. We ended up in the drug store part of the hospital. Then, there were counters and stools and sodas were served from a fountain. We were sitting on stools enjoying a drink when this obviously drunk guy sat on a stool next to my dad. This inebriated guy became loud in his conversation with dad. I was embarrassed.

Everyone was looking at dad and him and here I was sitting next to dad. The drunk ranted on and on and I had finally had enough embarrassment in front of my fellow student. I said to dad, "Let's get out of here. That drunk is causing everyone to stare at us."

Dad, without hesitation, looked me right in the eye and asked, "Do you know who that man is?"

I said, "No."

He replied, "I don't either, but he has been quoting 'The Lady of the Lake' and anyone who can do that, then allows himself to get in this state needs help. If you don't believe that you need to get out of medicine right now." Dad had made his point unquestionably.

A few alcoholics, when hung over from a bad binge and wanting to get sober; able to return to work, able to stop vomiting, and to become civil once again, would come to see me and they would invariably say, "If you help me get over this drunk this time, I'll never do it again. I promise! I mean it! I am going to quit for sure." Now, I've treated them like they were the greatest persons living and also like they were the lowest scum that walked, and places in between. It never mattered. Once I helped them become sober and over the DTs (Delirium tremens), it wouldn't be long until they were back with the same song, second verse, just like before. I just had no success. I eventually decided that I was just not a good doctor in these situations because they would always come back drunk.

One alcoholic's demise I shall never forget. He worked as a welder for a major company. He would end up in our clinic for a two to three day stay to get over the DTs, etc., about once every six to eight weeks. This went on year after year. He knew exactly the minute he was OK as far as eating and returning to work was concerned. He would sneak out of the clinic at night when no one was looking. Our nurse would call and say, "So-and-so's gone." He would tell us he was sorry but that he knew he was OK, so there was no need for him to stay longer. Later, we would hide his clothes to keep him from walking out on his own.

I often wondered why a company would keep working a guy like this. He was a union guy, but even so, he missed so much work because of his drinking problem it would have been no problem to let him go. The union wouldn't have a thing to say in reality.

I just called his plant and was able to talk to his foreman. I outright asked him why they continued to employ him. They were well aware that his problem was alcohol related because we had to write medical excuses for his absences. I told him that this had to be costly on their insurance program and there was no way for them to know when he would show up for work. His foreman was quite frank and to the point. He said, "He is by far the best welder I have. I'd rather have him here when he's here than any two others. That is why I keep him. He's a great welder." There was no doubt in his voice.

One morning at about ten o'clock, I was called and told there had been a bad wreck at a certain bridge in the county and was asked to come quickly. This same alcoholic had been trying to avoid being picked up by the police and was traveling at a high rate of speed. He had hit the abutment of the bridge, almost cutting his car in half. He was killed instantly I'm sure, for where one of his arms was almost severed, there was very little bleeding. His heart was not pumping blood after he hit the bridge. He was picked up by our local mortician and I returned to my office.

About an hour later I was called to come to his mother's house. I was told that she was so upset and that no one could even talk to her and that she needed a shot. On the way to her home I was wondering just what I would say or do. Normally, I felt like people needed to handle their grief in a manner that suited them. They had to do it their way, so to speak. I did not give any sedative via injection unless the one grieving asked for one so they could sleep. Anyway, during my drive it dawned on me that this guy had to have been a terrific burden to his mother and family. They had helped him over drunk after drunk and listened to his promises to quit. I wondered if deep down they even hated him.

Upon arriving and entering the house, I found his mother crying and talking in unattached sentences. I just blurted out, "Mrs. So-and-so you have been relieved of a great burden."

I have never seen such a sudden change in a person's behavior. She ceased crying and said in a quiet calm voice, "Dr. Vaughan, that was my baby boy."

I have never felt so small in my life. How could I have said that? Her near hysteria ended, however, and I left there feeling like less than two cents. I left a prescription for a mild tranquilizer if she desired to get it filled. I apologized to the family for my statement. They were kind to me and said they understood. His family and mother were seen by me numerous times in the years that followed. Evidently I had been forgiven for I was still their family doctor.

Observations of the alcoholic revealed to me that they were a breed unto themselves. They would lie time after time to get what they wanted. In spite of all this they possessed an innate caring and compassion. They would do anything to help you. If it were raining and you had to walk a few miles in the rain; they would walk with you just to keep you company. On one occasion one of my alcoholic patients demonstrated this generosity of spirit very well. My car drowned out when I drove through deep water during a downpour. This man saw me stranded. I had gotten out of my car to see what things looked like under the hood. He came up to me and said, "Dr. Vaughan, you are getting wet. Get back in your car. I'll see what I can do."

He insisted on me getting out of the rain while he stayed right there in the downpour. After looking things over he said, "Dr. Vaughan, I think your distributor is wet. If you have a dry hand-kerchief I think I can fix it." My wife was with me, and she had some Kleenex in her purse. She handed them to him. He took the cover containing wires off, spot dried things, and then said, "See if it will start." It did. I tried to pay him for his help but he would have none of that. He just walked off. This Good Samaritan later committed suicide because of family problems brought on by his drinking. His wife had recently divorced him. I believe he just became too depressed about all of his problems. We will never know for sure.

There were two other alcoholics in our town that would give you the shirt off their back when sober. They also committed suicide by a gunshot wound to their heads. The only one that I can think of that I dealt with medically who quit drinking, did it on his own without any medication. You see, in past years I had tried talking with them, referring them to Alcoholic Anonymous, to psychiatrists, and to their ministers. I used drugs such as Antabuse, which was supposed to make them sick if they drank alcohol. They found out quickly that if they did not take the pill for a couple of days the drinking did not bother them. Dr. Sid even had one of his alcoholic patients come to the office daily so one of the nurses could give him his Antabuse. She watched him put it in his mouth and swallow it. After not too long a time, this patient just did not show up. He is one of the two who later shot himself. Dr. Sid did not charge for this service, he just wanted to do all he could to help this guy help himself.

Now the one patient that did help himself and quit drinking cold turkey was an absolute surprise to me. I did not know that he was a daily drinker and that he began drinking vodka in early morning and continued to drink all day. He was a politician and a successful businessman. He came to the office one day just as I returned from lunch and caught me before I entered the office. He asked if I could see him right away.

His wife had told him she would not be home when he returned from work if he had not been to see me for help. She told him she had had enough. I would defy anyone to know he was a daily drinker of a considerable amount of alcohol. He did not smell of alcohol, talk strange, walk strange, work strange, or anything.

He had a pleasant personality and always a ready smile. I told him I would work him in.

He confided in me that recently he had been drinking more than he should and he wanted a complete physical. I said OK and did check him completely as well as drew blood for a multiple chemistry profile and a blood alcohol level. I wondered what his alcohol level would be about two o'clock in the afternoon. The next day when I received the results you could have floored me with a breath of air. It was 0.40 mgm%. Drunk driving in Tennessee was 0.10 mgm%. I could not believe my eyes. He had been a drinker for many years, and had increased his intake so gradually that he functioned well at that level. Even his liver function enzymes were not that bad. I'm sure very few knew he was this severe an alcoholic. I called his office and asked him to come to my office as the blood report was back and that we needed to talk. He ate well and took vitamins and obviously had a good liver. I let him know how flabbergasted I was that he functioned as well as he did with a blood level of 0.40 mgm%. I was very surprised that his brain function was as good as it was. I told him I wanted him to go to a physician that I knew who treated alcoholics, since I didn't feel good about my expertise in this area.

He replied, "No. I can quit on my own. My wife said she would leave me if I didn't and she and my family mean too much to me for me to continue drinking." He did quit and his wife said later that you couldn't hire him to take a drink. He and his wife both thanked me and I didn't do anything. He did it all. I just showed surprise in finding out about his drinking problem.

CHAPTER 44

"You Poor Boy"

House calls could come at any time of day or night. One such story that comes readily to mind is the time I made a house call around midnight to see an elderly lady. I had not been to bed prior to this call. I had delivered a baby and made another call before this one. As is usual in homes of the elderly, the room was quite warm to most folks, but to me felt just fine. After I had talked to her, I placed a thermometer in her mouth to take her temperature. I just leaned back in my chair to wait four or five minutes. My fatigue, combined with the warm room was so conducive to sleep that I just fell asleep sitting up in the chair.

The next thing I recall is her patting me on the hands saying, "You poor boy." She felt sorry for my having to be up so late and said so. In my opinion, no one is more appreciative of anything you do for them than the two generations prior to mine. I also found that they really hate to be trouble to you. The younger generation are just the opposite. You cannot do enough, quickly enough, or go to enough trouble to satisfy their needs. The younger they are, the more they want, and expressed appreciation is rare.

CHAPTER 45

Tradition

I have always been a person of tradition. For example, I always wore the same clothes at our "WynRea" holiday party each year. This consisted of a white shirt and a pastel blue tie that was adorned with a pewter tie ornament that I picked up in Oberammergau, Germany when Mother took her four children there in 1980 to see The Passion Play. I wore this maroon velour sweater with a V neck that would allow me to show off my tie ornament. I would wear navy blue or black trousers with black shoes, but this would be the only time of the year that I would wear the tie ornament and maroon sweater.

In 1984, mom called Violet and me, as well as my sister, Martha, and her husband to see if we could go to Greece on a tour cruise package. Naturally we let her know that we could. While there I bought a white Greek hat. I wear it once a year, and once a year only, and that is to the Munford Celebrate activities that is a tradition in Munford. Munford Celebrate is the second Saturday in September. The town is blocked off. Craft booths, music stages, food booths, dunk tanks, antique car show, helicopter and horse rides, political booths and the like are everywhere.

Its a fun day. You see scads of people you know. You visit with them, and you eat fried fish, barbecue, watermelon, hot dogs, pig skins, cotton candy, and all types of tasty things. I do not like wearing a hat, but in September it is usually sunny and hot. My Grecian hat was my thing for the day. My lack of hair made wearing a hat sensible. I kidded with folks that commented on my hat, that I was a "Greek sheik." From 1984 until 2002 I never missed a year wearing that hat to the celebration.

In 2002 when we were leaving to go to the celebration, I could not find my hat. I would mill about, seeing as many folks that I knew, as I could. When I was greeted by one of my patients, Bessie Cooper, she said, "I have been looking for that Greek hat all day, I just knew you and Violet would be at the celebration. Where's your hat?"

She remembered my hat. It is flattering for people to look for your hat, for if they see it, they know they will see you. Chalk up another reward for practicing medicine in the country.

Jackie Gleason would say, "How sweet it is."

CHAPTER 46

The Check

D r. Sid and I took our daily income home each day. Some people made their check out to Dr. Witherington, some made their check out to Dr. Vaughan, and others made theirs out to Munford Clinic. We each received half of the day's take. If a check was made out to me, I was given it as that part of my pay for that day. If it were made out to Dr. Witherington, he would receive it in his part. It didn't matter who received the Munford Clinic checks. This way we didn't have to forge each other's name to make our individual deposits. If we needed to forge the others name on the back of the check before we endorsed it, we did. The bank was aware of the way we did this. Each day I would receive my income via Munford Clinic checks, Dr. Hugh Vaughan checks, and cash. Some days I would receive a check made out to Dr. Witherington. This would happen when splitting the day's take could not be done otherwise.

On one particular day, a part of my daily take was a check. It had come in the mail for payment on account. It was made out to me for twelve dollars. I noticed in the bottom left part of this check on the line following "For," the boldly printed word, "NOTHING."

Obviously, this person was not pleased with whatever I did for that bill. I found this to be typical human nature in a small town. The people were always very candid.

CHAPTER 47

The Funniest Chief Complaint

One day, a patient I saw early in the day, presented himself in such a manner as to make me grin and chuckle a little, off and on all day. I would actually grin and almost laugh out loud when his complaint would come to mind. It went on all day. I actually felt some of my female patients might think I was grinning at them when I was examining them when this unusual complaint kept cropping up in my mind. It was very, very funny to me. Men would use various ways to inquire about their "manhood" to me, but nothing compared to this. Most of the time men would come to see you with some other complaint, and after you had finished with them, they would, as just an after thought, say, "By the way, my nature is not up to par. Do you have something to give me for this?" Most of the time, I thought it was why they came in to start with. They just did not want to admit they were not "manly."

This patient was about my age now (seventy-three) when I was about thirty-five years old. He was sitting in the exam room when I entered. I said to him, who I knew well, "Mr. X, what can I do for you today?"

He said right off, "Have you ever tried to shoot pool with a piece of rope?" The more I thought of it the funnier it got. Picture that in your mind, someone actually trying to shoot pool with a piece rope. He had made his complaint picturesque.

It occurred to me several times during the day while examining patients, and then I would catch myself grinning about it. Luckily, no one said anything that day when a grin would surface in the middle of their visit.

CHAPTER 48

Mushroom Tea

The history of the patient's disease or the reason for their visit to your office is the major factor in you being able to make a diagnosis. The history leads you to what lab work you need and lets you know how your physical exam must be very thorough to the system involved in their complaint. Other systems examined may be just a screening exam of that system. System examples are the nervous, the skeletal, the pulmonary, the vascular etc. A good history is so important.

Sometimes the manner in which a history is given to you reveals just how we are a part of what we hear, what we do, and our desire to find out for ourselves. This patient is a good example of that.

A young man, about seventeen, came to see me. He had a look of anxiety. I knew him quite well. His parents were my patients, we attended the same church, and we would bump into one another at the post office or the grocery store often. He got to the point quickly. He said, "Dr. Vaughan, I think I might have done something that I shouldn't and that it may kill me." The "it may kill me" gets your attention big time.

I said, "What in the world did you do?"

He said, "I was told that if you picked mushrooms out of a cow patty, boiled them in water to make a tea, then drink it, you would get a nice high like you would from morphine. I did this yesterday and then they (I never knew who "they" were) told me if I got the wrong kind of mushrooms it would kill me. I don't know whether I got the wrong kind or not. Do you think anything is going to happen to me?"

I relaxed as far as worrying about him is concerned, and just had fun with him the remainder of the visit. I said essentially, "George, (not his real name) I can't believe you would do a thing like that. Does your mom and dad know about this?"

He said, "You are not going to tell them are you?"

I said, "No, I'm just curious." He appeared as healthy as a horse. He looked like he ought to look, and the fact it happened yesterday, meant to me that if he were going to get sick from this experiment, he would have done so by now.

I was not absolutely sure that nothing would happen. I used my memory. It said to me that the ingestion of a toxic substance would probably show itself long before twenty-four hours had gone by. To let him know that he was right in coming to the office, I asked him to take everything off from his waist up, that I wanted to check him a little.

Everything I checked was normal. His blood pressure, pulse, heart rhythm and tones, lungs, and abdominal exam were all normal. He was told to get dressed.

Right or wrong, I did what I usually did when addressing a young patient's behavior. I, in my way, gave him a little fatherly advise. It went like this, "You don't need to be experimenting with anything to get a high. You know things like that are not good for you. You might get attached to some drug and become an addict. Be careful, don't let anyone talk you into doing something that you know you ought not to do."

I looked in my Merck Manual after he left. Toadstool mushroom poisoning makes you sick as a dog quick. Symptoms begin, "a few minutes to two hours after eating." Cow patty mushrooms were not mentioned.

I had lots of smiles after that. Every time we would meet, he'd grin, me too. Where else but a small town country practice would you have pleasure like this?

CHAPTER 49

Human Nature Advice

One of our patients was terminally ill with cancer. As with most people in this condition, he was gradually, over too long a time, becoming more and more debilitated. He had, associated with his disease, severe nausea that was a serious problem and not very responsive to treatment. Pain relievers just added to this nausea. It seemed he was constantly saying, "I'm so sick! I'm so sick! I'm so sick!" He would repeat this over and over again. This patient was in his eighties and not as acute mentally as he had been. His wife was in her eighties and had, for months, waited on him the best she could and had listened to his "I'm so sick" time and time again.

One day, while I was there trying to symptomatically give him some relief, he was ranting repeatedly this, "I'm so sick" bit. His wife just looked at him and matter of factly said, "Well, just vomit. You'll feel better." It sounded funny to hear her say that, but you know, a person usually does feel better after they vomit following nausea.

Human nature advice, but I don't think he felt better.

CHAPTER 50

The Most Unusual Foreign Body

One day a woman in her sixties and from a most prominent and well respected family arrived via a same-day appointment. She was a widow and a very attractive lady. She dressed well and with style. I know that she came to see her doctor out of pure fear and desperation. She was afraid something would happen to her if she did not correct a situation. This situation was not only embarrassing to the nth degree, but one that had potential, in her mind, to being quite serious; as well it would have been, if not corrected.

This is in essence what she said, "I have a problem and it is embarrassing, but I must tell you. I have a Vaseline jar in my vagina and I can't get it out." You could have floored me with a feather.

I had my nurse, Mrs. Johnson, prepare her for pelvic exam and sure enough, a Vaseline jar was in her vagina. The bottom of the jar was deep in her vagina and the top was open and at the entroitus (the opening of the vagina). It was no trouble to grasp the jar top with a thumb on the inside of the jar and a couple of fingers on the outside. But here was the catch. Pulling on the tight fitting jar just didn't cause it to slip out. There had been air displacement and there was a vacuum behind the bottom of the jar, preventing it from moving. I pulled rather firmly with no results. It's funny how things run through your mind. I thought to myself, *Surely you are not going to have to break the jar.*

There had to be a way. Taking a red robin catheter and sliding it between the jar and vagina to a distance past the bottom of the jar and then with a syringe forcing air though the catheter to eliminate the vacuum came to mind. You see, this type case was not talked about in medical school. I decided to try slipping a fore finger along the side of the jar as far as I could, then, leaving it there, try pulling the jar out with the other hand. How lucky can you be? Very lucky indeed. It worked! My finger let air slip in beside it as I pulled the jar out. It was one of those jars that was about two and a half inches in diameter and three inches deep.

She told me that she had the jar in her hand with Vaseline on her finger and that she was putting Vaseline on her hemorrhoid and the jar slipped out of her hand into the vagina. Somehow I just didn't buy that story for I saw no evidence of a hemorrhoid, but I never questioned her about it. I just told her she was all right now or something like that. I'm not sure whether Mrs. Johnson remembers what I said or not, but there is no doubt in my mind she remembers the event.

It was not uncommon for a woman to come and with no hesitation say, "OK doctor, get that tampax out of me. I can't feel it." Or some came in saying, "I don't know why, but for some reason I have developed a bad discharge and an odor. See what's going on." There would be a tampax, condom, or whatever. This lady was just my most unusual vaginal foreign body case.

CHAPTER 51

Airline Call

In 1980 my mother called me and asked if I could go to Europe for ten days. She wanted to take us (her four children) to see The Passion Play in Oberammergau, Germany. I had no idea she had enough money to take us to New York, let alone Germany. I said, "You bet." I never dreamed of going overseas to another continent. It just never entered my mind.

Time to go arrived. There were forty-two of us in the tour group. I flew from Memphis to Nashville, then on to New York. The remainder of the group boarded the plane in Nashville. In New York we boarded the largest plane I have ever seen. It seemed the interior was fifty yards long and it had about twelve or fourteen seats across the mid-section. It was one of those that had two decks in the front section of the plane. We became airborne late in the afternoon, and there was soon, as they say, water, water everywhere. No land in sight. This was a new experience for me. After about an hour and a half into the flight an airline steward questioned over the sound system, "Is there a doctor on board?" I believe at least twenty-five fingers pointed at me. I raised my hand. The steward asked me to follow him.

As I moved by seats to get to the isle I felt quite anxious. *Wonder what this will be? Will I have to tell them to return to New York if I think it is a heart attack or some other serious malady?* Flashes of what to do zip through your mind quickly. I certainly wished I would know what to do on the plane if I knew what the problem was. All eyes followed the steward and me to the back of the plane. There sat a lady with a towel on her face. The steward with her said, "She has a nose bleed. Can you help us?" What a relief. I had had lots of experience with these during my twenty-five years of practice. I recall only one noise bleed that I could not stop by packing. The otorhinolaryngologist I referred that patient to could not stop it by packing either. He had to give the patient a general anesthesia and get direct exposure to cauterize the vessel.

I told the steward to get some ice and place it in a wet cloth, and put it on her nose with a little pressure while we prepared things for packing. I informed her that we should do this and she was agreeable. I let her know that I was a general practitioner and that I felt we could control the bleeding by packing her nose.

I asked her if she had a good sense of humor. She said, "No." I had planned to comment to her if she had said yes, that women would do anything to get attention. In my mind, this would have been a little humorous and would relax the situation a bit. I forgot about saying that.

I asked the steward if they had cotton and KY jelly on board.

He said, "We have cotton, but no KY jelly."

"Do you have Vaseline?" I asked.

He said, "No."

I said, "Bring me some butter." It's amazing how the mind works. I normally would take a tight, rolled up piece of cotton, say little finger size, wet it with cold water then put a thin coat of KY jelly on it and pack the nose with that. Most of the time you pack both sides, so more pressure could be applied to the front of the nose and particularly to the septum. The KY jelly would let the packing slip out without sticking and restarting a nose bleed. I had never thought of using butter before, but now it just popped into my mind. I guess I knew that they would have butter on board.

This lady was not on a blood thinner, and had no serious medical history and appeared quite healthy. I was comfortable packing her nose. I buttered my packing strips lightly and packed each side. Her nose stopped bleeding. I sat there with her for about fifteen minutes and found out quickly why she did not have a good sense of humor. She was a Yankee; an upstate New Yorker. Northerners, in my opinion, just don't have the good humor sense that we southerners have.

I advised her to leave the packing in an hour at least, then slip it out, that more than likely nothing would happen. I told her I thought her nose would be fine, and I felt her bleed would not recur. I also let her know, that just in case you will worry about it recurring, it was OK to leave the packing in until we reached Frankfurt. She seemed fine, so I returned to my seat.

In about five minutes after I had seated myself, the stewards came marching down the isle with a red rose in a vase singing, "For he's a jolly good fellow." I was presented the rose. It is comforting when things work out well in medicine, yet it is quite humbling to be asked to perform before folks on a plane, especially for a country doctor that had hardly been anywhere. It flat reminds you of your limits when the possibilities are multiple.

This has a most pleasant and satisfactory ending. I was sitting in a different section of the plane on the return trip to New York from Amsterdam when a man walked down the isle toward me and stopped, looked at me, and said, "Are you the doctor that packed a woman's nose on the way to Frankfurt last Monday?"

I said, "Yes."

He said, "Would you please come up front, she wants to thank you again." She did.

Things like that make your day.

CHAPTER 52

The Heimlich Maneuver

Most everyone has heard of this maneuver that is applied to people who get their airway blocked by food, especially meat. The blockage of the airway will result in death if it is not removed. Those affected will show signs of desperation. They will begin to start grasping at their throat with their hands, get red faced, and then become cyanotic in the face (bluish, especially their lips).

While eating lunch with Violet at a cafeteria in Millington one Sunday, I was suddenly tapped on the shoulder and was told, "Dr. Vaughan, I think a man at that table needs you. He's choked." Buck Sigler had tapped my shoulder. He pointed to a nearby table with about eight people sitting there. He was not a member of the party but had just seen the man struggling and trying to breathe.

I quickly went to the table and asked the man, "Are you all right?" It was sort of a dumb question because appearances told me he was in trouble. He shook his head no. He was wide-eyed and anxious looking with a very red face and his lips were slightly bluish in cast. I reached around him from his back, locked my hands together, and jerked my hands into his upper abdomen. Nothing happened to change his status. I jerked again. He was still not breathing. Now, I am telling you, by now this was a nerve wracking situation.

These people did not know me from Adam. I don't believe I told them I was a doctor. I thought prayerfully, *Don't let this guy die!* Someone walked up and said they had called 911 and that medics would be there soon. I had never used this maneuver, never even seen it done. Many thoughts ran through my mind in a very few seconds. Things like, *Maybe, I will have to do a tracheotomy.* I had never done this either or even seen it done, though I believe I could do it if I had to.

Anyway, after the second pump was unsuccessful, I decided to pump again really hard and did. Lucky me and lucky patient. A large bolus of beef came up in his mouth. Violet grabbed it and a breath was taken by this man. All was OK. I advised the man and his family he should go to an emergency room and have a chest x-ray to make sure he had no small bronchial blockage anywhere.

Very shortly after that, the medics ran in with a stretcher. I don't know how the medics felt, but I was always relieved when I was called to an emergency situation, and arrived there only to find no emergency. Life threatening emergencies are anxiety producing to a physician as well as the patient and their family. At least they always were to me.

Once again, I advised the man who had been choked to let the medics take him to the emergency room, just to be evaluated. He would have no part of it and said emphatically, "I'm OK. I am going to finish eating." I would guess him to have been near seventy years old. I had not seen him or any of his family before and never saw any of them afterwards.

This sort of thing shakes you up a bit. All of this happened in a wide open cafeteria where forty or fifty people were eating. I think I ate a little more before we left but, I had lost my appetite. I was lost in my thoughts of, *What if?* Another thing about this situation which will be hard to believe is that neither the man nor any of his family even said as much as thank you to me.

CHAPTER 53

"Thank You Jesus!"

I am not a gambler, as such, yet I do bet a buck on a football or basketball game. I bet a dime on scats, or a double scat on birdies in golf. I might enter a pool on the ending and score of the World Series. My bets are for fun and engagement such that if all were like me, there never would have been a need for a casino. That lets you know that this bet is just an unscientific belief that may or may not be 100% accurate, but I'd bet that doctors who deliver babies in the south would agree with the following observations by a substantial majority.

There are certain characteristics or responses that have seemed to me in my career as unique to the Afro-American race. I'll mention those that are associated with pregnancy and labor / delivery.

There are some who crave red clay dirt when they are pregnant, and they do not hesitate to eat it. I have been told this is because they lack certain vitamins or minerals, and are anemic. I doubt that explanation, for after you give them a good prenatal capsule that contains vitamins, minerals, and iron they continue to nibble on dirt.

Another characteristic of this ethnic group is that they, in general, are easier to encourage to push with uterine contractions after they are completely dilated and nearing delivery. They seem to expect to have some pain and are not expecting to come into the hospital in labor, be put under, and wake up happy with a newborn. They expect to help themselves by pushing with contractions. They know this will make them make progress faster. It does.

Now the big item here comes just after delivery of their new-borns. When you tell an Afro-American woman they have a new boy or new girl they say (I believe eighty-five to ninety percent of the time) two or three times in rapid fire succession, "Thank you Jesus, thank you Jesus, thank you Jesus!" They do this and single or married makes no difference.

CHAPTER 54

An Afro-American Trait

You have to go a long way to beat black humor and their manner of speaking in the South. Dr. Sid hired a young black man to work for him at what ever job he needed done, such as driving for his wife, mowing the lawn, painting, etc. His name was Jess L. Payne. He would spend a lot of afternoons playing with Dr. Sid's son, Albert Sidney Witherington III, when "Little Sid" was five to eight years old. They would throw the football, play tag, bat the baseball, and the like.

One afternoon I got a break and decided to go to the drug store for some ice cream. Just as I walked out the back door of the clinic and started toward Wooten's Pharmacy (walking between the clinic and Dr. Sid's house) a young black boy, perhaps a little younger than Jess L., walked up to him and said, "Jess L., loan me two dollars."

Jess L. reached into his pocked, pulled out his wallet, picked out two ones, and handed it to this boy. After this young guy left, I said to Jess L., "Who was that? I don't know him."

Jess L. said, "I don't know his name."

I said, "What do you mean you don't know his name, you just loaned him two bucks."

Jess L. said, "I know where he stays."

That is typical. Their manner of speech and not telling or ratting on one another is, it appears, an unwritten law with blacks. If a black person comes in with a rather severe knife cut or a gunshot wound, and you ask, "Who did this to you?"

They will say, in effect, " I don't know that person." This will be the answer even if they were gambling in the same card or dice game together. It appears to me that they protect their own color.

Another example of this same thing happens not too infrequently. Each community in the Munford area has a section of town where Afro-Americans live. It usually has a name. Jamestown is one of these community areas. I received a call requesting a house call to see an Afro-American that lived in one of these areas near Brighton. Dr. Sid and I made house calls to see anyone that needed our services that way. It was about nine-thirty at night, and was not a moonlit night.

I was not sure just which house this patient lived in, so after I arrived in the housing project area I was looking for house numbers. None could be seen. About that time a young boy that appeared to be fifteen years old, came walking down the street. I lowered my passenger widow and said, "I'm looking for Mrs. Mary Jones' house, can you tell me where she lives?"

He said, "I don't know her. She doesn't live around here."

I said, "Young man, I'm Dr. Vaughan, they called for me to make a house call to see her; that she was sick, and that she lived right in this area."

He hesitated a few seconds then said, "You know, I just happened to think, I believe a lady by that name lives in the second house on the right."

Same song second verse. One cold, rainy night at about eleven. Violet and I were playing canasta with my brother Bill and his wife, Marge. The phone rang. Dr. Sid's sister called me to see if I could make a house call to see an Afro-American lady that lived on her place. I said, "Sure."

She said, Hugh, "I hate to tell you this, but they live on the hill just about a quarter of a mile down the dirt road from my house. You will have to park on the road and walk up the hill. Its too muddy and slick for you to drive up to the house." She continued, "Her son said she was having chest pain, and they thought she was having a heart attack or I wouldn't have even called you to come out on a night like this." It was a blistering, cold, rainy night and the wind just made it miserable out.

I said, "Bill, come on and go with me on this house call."

He said, "OK." It was about ten miles to this house and Peggy (Dr. Sid's sister) was right, you never would have gotten a car up that muddy, rutted hill. I used my otoscope (light to look into ear canal) as a flashlight to try and see the best way for us to walk up to the house. They did not have a porch light on. The rain, wind, and coldness of the night was quite chilling, but we finally arrived at the house. When we entered the house, an Afro-American man in his thirties with a towel in front of his mouth said, "My mother's there in front of the stove, she is the one with chest pain." There was a pot belly stove near the back of the room. She was sitting in a rocking chair in front of the stove. He then said, "While you are here, I want you to look at me too." He dropped the towel down and revealed a large cut of his upper lip and face.

This type thing always rang a bell. He was the one that needed to be seen. They knew I would not go on a call to sew up a cut, but would come on a call to see someone with heart problems. They were afraid to try and drive the curvy, muddy road in their old car. He had been hit in the mouth with a beer bottle at the local bar lounge in nearby Mason, Tennessee. Mason was a regular night spot for blacks on Saturday night and this was Saturday night. I did question and talk to the lady, even examined her a little. It was obvious to me she was used as an excuse to get me there. This was a different son than the one that got Peggy to call me.

Bill, this guy, and I made our way to the car on this miserable night and went to the clinic. I repaired his laceration. He said, "You are going to take me home aren't you?"

I said, "You must be kidding. You can call someone to come and get you now or sit in the waiting room until daylight and then call someone."

The black culture is very knowledgeable in knowing how to get things done for themselves. The diversities in people, and the human nature of the cultures, add a big plus to practice in the country.

CHAPTER 55

"That Ain't Nothing"

O ur waiting room was square. One corner was a boxed off, rectangle shaped receptionist area. This area had a counter top. The area was about five feet by twelve feet. The entire room was like twenty feet by twenty feet. Chairs lined the walls and back to back seats occupied the center section. Three employees sat behind the boxed off area. They could readily see all in the waiting room and vice versa. They could talk back and forth, for the boxed area did not go to the ceiling and was not glassed in. Visitation with our employees went on more than it probably should have, but this made coming to the office pleasant, so to speak. It sure made the waiting-to-be-seen time go faster. There were eighteen or twenty places for patients to sit. Our receptionist, book keeper, and insurance lady sat behind the counter.

People would read, talk, and gaze around. When Dr. Sid or I would buzz the receptionist to send the next patient, the receptionist would just call the next patient's name and say, "You may go back to Dr. Vaughan's office (or Dr. Sid's)."

Women, in the early years of my practice, usually wore a dress to the office. I suppose, most of us, at one time or another, has worn underclothes that were too big for us, or at least the elastic was worn out. You know how you will wrap a towel around your waist when naked, roll the top part on itself, then tuck it under so it will be snug and not slip. If the rolled up part did become unrolled or untucked the towel would fall flat to the floor.

On this particular day, our waiting room was crowded and a lady that was wearing a dress had just been called to go to my office. She immediately stood up to start toward my office and her bloomers (the longer panties that you don't see at all now) fell right down to the floor. She just reached down, pulled them up, and said as she looked straight forward, "That ain't nothing."

That's human nature. What better could she have said?

CHAPTER 56

Voice Recognition

Country medicine is rewarding daily. The one on one relationships regarding medical problems with the search for the diagnosis is a pleasant challenge that is so satisfying when you establish just what the problem is. It's like finding the pieces to a puzzle that makes the picture complete. When you can establish a diagnosis, the treatment is a piece of cake. If you don't know what to do for a specific diagnosis, it's quite easy to look this up in your books. This you experience every day. Added to that pleasure is the personality relationships. People are different, interesting, and add a dimension to your life that is immeasurable.

You never know just what people will remember about you as they encounter you as their physician. For example, while on vacation in Venice, Florida for the month of January in 2003, I was going through a flea market where all types of crafts were sold. Kitchen ware, tools of all sorts, and the handy use items are everywhere. You can see lots of golf equipment, golf hats, and over production golf balls with logos for sale at a reasonable rate. You name it, they have it, everything from pet rocks up.

It was here that a lady made my day. I was getting ready to purchase a pair of small size ice cube tongs. I asked the sales lady if they could be used to pick up olives if you were serving them as an hors d'oeuvre

She said "Yes."

Just then a woman touched my right shoulder from behind me. I turned her way, she said, "I'm Jackie."

I said, "I beg you pardon."

She said, "I'm Jackie McKay" (*not her real name*).

This didn't ring a bell with me and I did not recognize her. I felt she had mistaken me for someone else. I said, "I'm sorry but..."

She interrupted me and said, "You packed my nose when you were in the condo next to ours. Don't you remember? I recognized your voice; then when I saw you, I knew it was you."

I said, "I didn't know I had that distinctive a voice."

She said, "After all, you are not from New Jersey." The Tennessee accent must have a certain ring to it. This packing of her nose happened two years ago and I had never thought about it ever happening. I had not seen her or her husband before our meeting two years ago, and had not seen them since.

I had met them as we would come and go from our entrances to the condos. The natural greetings of, "Good morning," took place. You get around to, "Where are you from?" at these meetings. Later it's, "What do you do?" or "Are you retired and what did you do before you retired?" I had told them I was a general practitioner before I retired in 1998.

Several nights later, at about ten o'clock , there was a knock on our front door. It was Mr. McKay. He said, "Would you mind taking a look at my wife. She is experiencing a nose bleed." I ended up packing her nose and was able to stop the active bleeding which was more active than most nose bleeds. She left the packing in the rest of the night and removed it after getting up the next morning. When the bleed recurred, she went to the emergency room, where she was referred to an ENT physician. He had to cauterize the bleeder.

It is so satisfying for people to approach you and say thanks for small favors. She said she thought about us often. She insisted it was my voice that caught her attention. So you see, people may remember you by your voice.

CHAPTER 57

Conclusion Thoughts

There have been dramatic changes in our country since my childhood and during my adult years. Some have benefited society immensely, yet others, in my opinion, have caused a marked degradation in society. These changes will be commented upon briefly under separate headings. I am so thankful I had the opportunity to practice medicine when I did. The early years of my practice were the best. It was the golden years of medicine, that is, during an era where patients looked up to their doctors and the doctors looked upon his patients as extended family. Patients expected you to tell them what you thought and, by and large, they accepted what you told them as law. Their trust in you as their physician was overwhelming. Your judgment was rarely questioned. After governmental intervention into medicine via Medicare and Medicaid things changed.

CHAPTER 58

Social and Economic Changes

Since I began practice in 1955, changes here have been many and I believe, over all, have caused a degradation of character and integrity. The 'whatever feels good' attitude has led to the acceptance of social mores that I feel are causing a deterioration of society as a whole. There seems to be a growing number of individuals that make up our society that have no standard of morality. Examples are: The acceptance of marriage not being a requirement to live together as man and wife. "Living in" is not frowned upon these days. Homosexuality has become a legal norm (one cannot discriminate against because of sexual orientation). Pedophilia may be accepted as a normal sexual orientation if things continue like they are going.

Honesty is not a needed character trait under certain circumstance (Clinton and Monica Lewinsky). Lying under oath in a federal court of law is not considered a felony by the United States Senate if it concerns sex, as a former President of the US demonstrated in a federal court. Quotas and affirmative action, though both discriminate because of race, are believed by many, to be the right thing to do. Adultery is accepted as an "everyone does it" thing.

Single parenthood is widely accepted and is rewarded by stipends from the federal government. It was common for unwed, teenage girls to come into my office for their pregnancy confirmation exam, so "I can get my check started." It was like, "I'm entitled. I'm in school, not married and pregnant so I deserve taxpayers money." These changes are not a part of the golden years. These scenarios seemed to start after the Medicare and Medicaid programs began.

The welfare programs of our government are leading us straight toward socialism. We are, via governmental social programs, being told you don't have to be responsible, you are entitled to the benefits of another's labor. You are deserving of food, shelter, medical care and child support whether you earn it or not. Medicaid and the WIC program are examples. Responsible people are being penalized and irresponsible people are being rewarded. You can get pregnant and get a check, or get pregnant and get an abortion at taxpayers expense. Death intentionally, of the unborn child via abortion, is not considered murder in our culture.

The alternative lifestyle of live-ins is everywhere. The male may have a great job and earn a tremendous salary, yet his live-in mate and their child or children will be on Medicaid and receive food stamps for she is not working. They may live in a nice home and drive two cars. The female of the house may stay home, raise the children on governmental stipends, and receive medical care at taxpayers expense via Medicaid. You see, less income tax is paid this way and the medical insurance for the family would cost much more if they were married. The employer of the male spouse would be deducting more from the male's check, if they were married, for medical insurance. I knew of five cases like this in the little town of Munford, Tennessee. Project that nationwide. The more social programs we have, the closer to socialism we become. These problems were not a part of the golden years.

Whether we want to admit it or not, we had as president of the United States, a man that seemed to have no respect for the rule of law, or the presidency itself. He lied in a federal court of law, showed no respect for the White House, Air Force One, the Lincoln bedroom, or his wife and child, in my opinion. I believe this lack of morality in the President of the United States is catching. We are, in most cases, taught to respect the President. Leadership commands a following.

Federal programs and grants in all phases of life are present in many other fields such as agriculture, art, etc. I could comment on how I think these are not good in the long run as well as stepping stones towards a Marxist type government. I am mentioning these things only to show that morals, as a factor, seem not to be considered at all.

Morals are important for good health mentally, which also affects the physical, in my opinion.

CHAPTER 59

Medical Changes

The advancements in the medical field in my life time have been so dramatic and so beneficial that books could be written about this alone. Statements to hit the high spots will be used.

Antibiotics discovered. Polio vaccine discovered. Measles, mumps, and chicken pox vaccine discovered. The heart lung machine discovered. (The heart lung machine has enabled cardiac surgery of all types to be performed.) By-pass cardiac vessel surgery, cardiac valve replacement, heart transplants are examples (vascular surgery in general was in its early stages while I was in medical school). Carotid artery surgery is another example.

The CAT scan came into being. The MRI invented. Plastic surgery advancements are innumerable. Arthroscopic surgery introduced. Laser surgery introduced. DNA discovered. Gene relationships to many diseases discovered. New blood chemistry testing available. This list could go on and on.

It is incomprehensible the advancements that have been made in medicine since I started practice. Drugs and their uses have not even been mentioned...

CHAPTER 60

High Tech Things

Technology in all fields has advanced beyond imagination during my life. The atom bomb. The calculator. The computer. The Internet. The laser beam. Power steering and brakes. Space travel with landings on the moon. The space station. The weedeater. The pneumatic hammer. The crow's nest for high wire uses and limb cutting. The jet engine for airplanes. These are just a few of many technological advances. It is mind boggling just to think about them.

CHAPTER 61

Summary of Conclusion

The changes in the medical field and the technological field are benefits to society as a whole.

There is a big exception to me. After governmental intervention into the medical field via Medicare and Medicaid, things began to change. Since that time the field of medicine has become sick and this sickness is a chronic illness. It has no cure in the foreseeable future that I can see. The respect for doctors has steadily gone down hill. Respect for people in other fields has been riding the same train down a slippery slope. No one seems to trust anyone anymore.

The adoption of our governmental social, economical programs has for the most part been detrimental to society, from this country doctor's point of view. The absence of moral standards is detrimental to society in my opinion. I agree with Dr. Kenneth McFarland, who was a nationally known speaker. He was the Superintendent of Public Schools in Topeka, Kansas. He later devoted his time to public speaking on liberty under law, Americanism, and the greatness of the free and competitive enterprise system. He says in essence, "Anytime you do for others what they should be doing for themselves, you do not help them, you hurt them." He says this is not Christian charity.

His statements about our nation are appropriate to our trend toward socialism and to us as individuals. Dr. McFarland (now deceased) was worried about this great nation being replaced by another form of government than the one our founding fathers created. He and his associates were not worried about our country being destroyed by an atomic bomb or from an attack from without. They were afraid it would be replaced from within. This would occur because we adopted the philosophy, "That we are no longer responsible for our own economic welfare, nor are we responsible for our own moral conduct."

It is my wish that we as a people in this great nation will reflect upon the past and learn from it. May we see that the governmental control of things does not necessarily mean betterment or progress. May we seek to be responsible for our own economic welfare and our own moral conduct. May we know that we deserve the results of our actions, good or bad.

I hope you, as a reader of this book, know that I am blessed to have been a country doctor, and that I am blessed to have practiced where I did, when I did, and am fortunate to have been born in America. Life has been good to me.

I am grateful.

To order additional copies of

My Life
as a
Country Doctor

Please visit our web site at
www.pleasantword.com

Also available at:
www.amazon.com
and
www.barnesandnoble.com

Printed in the United States
35064LVS00005B/70-1008